Dae Ye Min' Langsyne?

Dae Ye Min' Langsyne?

A Pot-pourri of Games, Rhymes and Ploys of Scottish Childhood

Collected and Edited
by
Amy Stewart Fraser

Illustrations
by
Constance and Brian Dear

Routledge & Kegan Paul
London and Boston

First published in 1975
by Routledge & Kegan Paul Ltd
Broadway House, 68–74 Carter Lane,
London EC4V 5EL and
9 Park Street,
Boston, Mass. 02108, USA
Set in Linotron Bembo
and printed in Great Britain by
T. & A. Constable Ltd
© Amy Stewart Fraser 1975
No part of this book may be reproduced in
any form without permission from the
publisher, except for the quotation of brief
passages in criticism

ISBN 0 7100 8233 9

Contents

Contents

Letter to Contributors

Carlisle
1974

Dear Friends,

Of making many books there is no end, we are told, and that goes for books on children's games. In the past a vast amount of research has been carried out on this fascinating subject.

This book, I confess, entailed little research. It has grown out of endless conversations, and over a hundred and sixty letters from you who were, at the outset, strangers, but whom now I regard as my friends. It contains only personal recollections, yours and mine.

You wrote to tell me what you recollect of your own happy childhood, and what you learned from your parents and grandparents.

Letters which obviously gave you great pleasure to write, and were a delight to read, came pouring in, not only from many parts of Britain, but from South Africa and Canada, Pennsylvania, California and the Channel Islands.

They came from Bearsden and Buckie, Fochabers and Fintry, Inverbervie and Tillypronie, Keith and Cummertrees, from Orkney and Shetland, from

> Edinburgh, Leith,
> Portobello, Musselburgh, and Dalkeith,

from

> Aiberdeen and twal' mile roon,
> Fife, an' a' the lands aboot it.

and a score of other places.

Letter to Contributors

From you Over-Seventies, Eighties, and Nineties came memories of your toys and ploys, your capers and customs, and Red Letter Days; songs and games came also from younger generations.

Here they are, then, just as you described them, with your own comments. I do hope you enjoy seeing them in print.

Thank you again for your cheerful collaboration; I hope the collection will revive happy memories for all its readers, particularly the memories of those who left Scotland at an early age, and whose recollections of their homeland are inextricably bound up with their childhood years, and with the games they once played at home.

Amy Stewart Fraser

Acknowledgments

I offer grateful thanks to the following Scots who contributed memories of their childhood; without their help this project could not have been completed:

James Affleck
E. I. Alexander
Janet M. S. Allan
Eleanor Anderson
Jane Anderson
Nora Arnott
G. S. Barton
Simon Berry
Ellie M. Berwick
Elsie J. Black
Elizabeth B. Boag
Jean Boag
M. M. Borthwick
M. Murray-Bowser
Margaret Brander
Robert Burns Brands
Lilias Britton
M. Brocklehurst
Charlotte Burnett
William Burns
M. Cameron
Colin Campbell
Mabel Campbell
Edward Clark

Peter Clark
J. H. C. Clarke
Margaret Clarke
Sheila Clay
F. H. Clift
R. T. S. Cluness
Malcolm J. Cockburn
Ian L. Cormack
Graham K. Cox
I. M. Crawford
Elsa Cunningham
N. L. Currie
Nan Davidson
Alison Devlin
Eleanor M. Dewar
A. G. Dunbar
Elizabeth Duncken
Flora Edmunds
Anna English
E. M. Erskine
Maggie Fleming
Jean Forbes
Elsie J. Forrest
Edith Forsyth

David A. Fraser
Neil and Marguerite Fraser
Mark and Alena Fraser
Dorothea H. Fyfe
Janet Garvey
D. Graham
James Grant
Henry R. Gray
A. Grieve
Mary Hall
Flora Hardy
Ena Hart
Edith Hossack
D. Hunter
Helen Ireland
Catherine B. Johnston
Elizabeth Kennedy
John Kerr
Marian Laird
G. Lawton
Adziel Lillie
Grace Linford
Mary W. Little
Iain and Rosamond Jex-Long
Marjory Lyell
Norman Lynn
Ray MacCulloch
G. S. Mackay
Mary P. Mackie
George M. Maltman
Margaret Marshall
J. M. Mason
C. Massey
James Mateer
Ena Melross
Helen Melvin
Alice H. Miller
Harry R. Milne
Elsie F. Moffat
James Mort

J. Munro
David D. Murison
Margaret McCulloch
Dorothy C. Macdonald
F. M. McDowall
Ina MacGregor
Flora M. McIntosh
Isabella Mackenzie
Millicent McLellan
Elizabeth C. G. MacSween
J. F. Munro
Leah Neal
M. Neillie
Tom and Sheila Newlands
A. B. Nicol
M. L. Nicoll
Freda Paterson
E. Patterson
J. Pahl
F. Muriel Pekle
Emily B. B. Potts
C. Purcell
Mina Ramage
Agnes K. Riley
Mary A. Robb
Margaret Robbie
E. B. S. Robertson
John Robertson
Jim Rodgers
Mary C. Rogerson
Mary Rose
Patricia Ross
Caroline Rothnie
Edith Roy
Charlotte Rutherford
Margaret M. Sandison
Ann Scott
J. Scott
H. D. Shepherd
Anna Smith

Acknowledgments

Elizabeth Smith

Louisa Smith

Walter M. Spiers

J. Lindsay Steele

Betty M. Stewart

R. Stewart-Wilson

Sheila M. Streatfield

Jessie Stuart

Augusta Sutherland

Stella Sutherland

Jack S. Swan

Janet S. Tait

Saul Taylor

Elizabeth Thomson

Leslie Thomson

R. W. Turner

Sadie Veitch

Grace Walker

Effie F. Ward

Margaret L. Wells

Mary Whelpdale

Margaret Whitehead

Harriet Wilson

Janet Yeates

I offer my special thanks to Elspeth Fraser for much encouragement and practical help; to J. K. Annand for permission to quote his bairn-rhymes from *Sing it Aince for Pleisure*, which appear on pp. 29, 140, 184 and 200; to Mrs R. T. S. Cluness and Messrs Robert Hale and Company for permission to quote from *The Shetland Isles* by Andrew T. Cluness; and to the daily newspapers and periodicals who kindly printed my appeal for readers' recollections.

Some Books Consulted

CARSWELL, CATHERINE, *The Scots Weekend*, George Routledge & Sons, London, 1936.

CLUNESS, ANDREW T., *The Shetland Isles*, Robert Hale, London, 1951.

DOUGLAS, RONALD MACDONALD, *The Scots Book*, Alexander Maclehose, London, 1935.

McNEILL, F. MARIAN, *The Scots Kitchen*, Blackie, Glasgow, 1931.

Dedicated to Scotland's Bairns,
Old and Young,
Everywhere

In order that you may, in the Scottish sense,
'mind' anything, there must be something to
'mind', and then the mind to 'mind' it.

John Ruskin

Lang, Lang Syne

Here are the words of that old song we all sang in our childhood. Dae ye min' how often it appeared on the programme at Sorees! It dates from the latter years of the nineteenth century, and from it I have chosen the title of this collection of memories.

D'ye min' langsyne,
When the simmer days were fine,
When the sun it shone far brichter than it's ever dune sin'
    syne?
D'ye min' the ha'brig turn,
Where we guddled in the burn,
An' were late for the schule in the mornin'?

D'ye min' the sunny braes
Where we gathered hips an' slaes,
An' fell amang the bramble busses, tearin' a' oor claes;
An' for fear we micht be seen,
We cam slippin' hame at e'en,
An' got lickit for oor pains in the mornin'.

D'ye min' the miller's dam,
When the frosty winter cam',
Hoo we slade across the curlers' rink, an' made their
    game a sham;
When they chased us through the snaw,
We took leg-bail ane an' a',
But we did it ower again in the mornin'.

What famous fun was there,
At oor games at 'hounds and hare',
An' we played the truant frae the schule because it was the
  Fair;
When we ran frae 'Patie's Mill' thro' the wuds on
  Whinnyhill,
An' were thrashed wi' the tawse in the mornin'.

Noo oor youth's sweet spring is past,
An' oor autumn's come at last;
Oor simmer day has passed away, oor winter's comin'
  fast;
But though lang the nicht may seem,
May we sleep withoot a dream
Till we wauken on yon bricht Sabbath mornin'.

George James Laurie, DD

The Bairnie's Ups and Downs

> Shoo shuggie, ower the glen,
> Mammy's pet an' Daddy's hen.

It has been said that rhymes enter our lives with the first lullabies we hear, and more and more rhymes follow as we grow older. It was usually when lulling a new baby to sleep, either up in her arms or down in his cradle, that old forgotten lullabies came unbidden to a mother's lips.

I learned the following lullaby from hearing my mother sing it to my baby sister. It dates back to 1858, at least.

> Hush-a–ba birdie, croon, croon,
> Hush-a–ba birdie, croon,
> The sheep are gane tae the silver wood
> An' the kye are gane tae the broom, broom.
>
> An' it's braw milkin' the kye, kye,
> It's braw milkin' the kye,
> The birds are singin', the bells are ringin',
> The deer come gallopin' by, by.
>
> An' hush-a–ba birdie, croon, croon,
> Hush-a–ba birdie, croon,
> The lads are gane tae the mountain high
> An' they'll no' be hame till noon, noon.

Ba-la-loo was a Scots lullaby in the time of King James VI, if not at a much earlier period; the words were used in a number of lullabies, one of the best-known being the Baroness

1

Nairne's Cradle Song, 'Can ye sew cushions?', which I first heard sung by Miss Waterston in 1906, in Edinburgh.

Can ye Sew Cushions?

O can ye sew cushions?
An' can ye sew sheets?
An' can ye sing ba–la–loo
When the bairnie greets?
An' hie an' baw birdie,
An' hie an' baw lamb,
An' hie an' baw birdie,
Ma bonnie wee lamb!

> Heigh O, heugh O, what'll I dae wi' ye?
> Black's the life that I lead wi' ye,
> Mony o' ye, little for tae gie ye,
> Heigh O, heugh O, what'll I dae wi' ye.

Hush a baw lammie,
An' hush-a-baw dear,
Hush-a-baw lammie,
Yer minnie is here.
The wild win' is ravin',
Yer minnie's hert's sair,
The wild win' is ravin'
But ye dinna care.

> Heigh O, heugh O, what'll I dae wi' ye, etc.

Sing ba–la–loo, lammie,
Sing ba–la–loo, dear,
Does wee lammie ken
That his daddie's no' here?
Ye're rockin' fu' sweetly,
On minnie's warm knee,
But daddie is rockin'
Upon the saut sea.

> Heigh O, heugh O, what'll I dae wi' ye, etc.

Shetland mothers within living memory had a hard life. The father of the family was often at sea five days out of seven, so the mother had to work the croft, cast the peats and bring

2

them home in a creel on her back, look after the cow, the pig, and the hens, and care for her growing family, but she found time to sing tender little songs to her peerie mootie lammie, as in this fragment which I heard sung in 1894:

> Hushaba, my curry ting,
> Cuddle close ta mammie,
> Cuddle close an' hear me sing
> Peerie mootie lammie.

Stella recalled this Bressay cradle-song:

> Baloo, balilo, baloo, balilo
> Baloo, balilo, baloo, balilo.
> Gae awa' peerie fairies
> Fae wir peerie bairn.
>
> Baloo, balilo, baloo, balilo
> Baloo, balilo, baloo, balilo,
> Dan come bonnie angels
> Ta wir peerie bairn.
>
> Baloo, balilo, baloo, balilo
> Baloo, balilo, baloo, balilo,
> Dey'll sheen ower da cradle
> O' wir peerie bairn.
> Baloo, balilo, baloo, balilo.

And Elizabeth remembered that in Bigton, while rocking the infant, they sang

> Row ta boats ta Mailie
> Ship anunder sailie,
> Row fast, row slow,
> Brakk da boats at winna row,
> At winna row ta Mailie.

Flora gave me this charming trifle:

> Peerie mootie, peerie mootie,
> O du love, du joy, du beauty,
> Whar is du come far, an' whar is du been?

and also this lullaby from the Norwegian of Nordahl Grieg:

Nicht ita da Nort is lang
Maamie sings a sleepy sang
Caald he mirkens ower da sea,
Peerie licht, come ta me.

Caald-rife wis da day at's geen,
Sheenin blue dy boannie een,
Laek da flooer closin noo,
Peerie licht, sleep due.

Morning brings nae sun-blink here
Nane ava bit dee, my dear,
By name bit dee my hert is aesed,
Peerie licht, waaken plaesed.

A Buchan mother sang:

Cuddle in yer beddie-baa
An' get a bonnie sleepie-o,
An' I'll awa' tae milk the coo
An' gie tae her a neepie-o!

And in the Border Counties they still murmur

Hush ye, hush ye, little pet ye,
Hush ye, hush ye, dinna fret ye,
The Black Douglas sall not get ye.

These lines are from a lullaby said to have been sung to their children by women of the English garrisons during the War of Independence.

In my childhood in the 1890s I saw many a babe in its rocking-cradle, swathed in blankets like a cocoon, with a criss-cross pattern of cord which was passed through rings on the side of the cradle and held the infant firmly in position while it was being rocked. In those days the following cradle-song was familiar. (The rocking-cradle with its wooden hood has had its day and is now a collector's item.)

The Fidgety Bairn

Hush, my dear, the gallopin' men
Ride thro' the bracken and ride owre the ben,

4

Mammy'll watch her sleepin' hen,
So close your e'en, my dearie!

Close your e'en an' greet nae mair,
O but your mither's hert is sair,
Daddy's asleep i' the big rockin' chair,
So close your e'en, my dearie!

O but will ye never learn, never learn, never
learn?
Ne'er, ne'er was sic a bairn, sic a bairn, sic a
bairn!
Brakin' ma hert, ye fidgety bairn, fidgety bairn,
fidgety bairn!
So close your e'en, my dearie!
Close — your — e'en — my dearie!

Scotland is rich in rhymes and sayings for the distraction of greetin' bairns. 'There's a black doggie on your back', a Deeside mother might tell her bairn, and amazingly the child would stop girnin' to try to get a glimpse of the little black dog; then she might tuck him into bed while singing:

'Hap an' row the feetie o't,
Hap an' row the feetie o't,
I never kent I had a bairn
Until I heard the greetie o't.'

Banffshire bairns sang to the baby in his cradle . . .

The cattie rade tae Passelet, tae Passelet, tae Passelet,
The cattie rade tae Passelet upon a harrow-tine, O!
'Twas on a weetie Wednesday, Wednesday, Wednesday,
'Twas on a weetie Wednesday I missed it aye sin' syne, O!

Or they would pat the soles of the baby's feet with the palm of the hand while singing:

Lucy Locket had a pocket
Guess ye fat wis in't,
Sugar bools an' wee toadstools,
That wis fat wis in't.

5

To accompany dandling there is a little song which I heard in Stirling over sixty years ago:

Dance to your daddie
My bonnie laddie,
Dance to your daddie,
My bonnie lamb!

Ye shall have a fishie
On a little dishie,
Ye shall have a herring
When the boats come hame!

Dance to your daddie
My bonnie laddie,
Dance to your daddie
My bonnie lamb!

Ye shall have a coatie,
An' a pair o' breekies,
Ye shall have a whippie
An' a supple Tam!

Jean's grandfather in Edinburgh dandled her on his knee while chanting

Dancety, diddlety, poppety pin,
Have a new dress when Summer comes in,
When Summer goes out it's all worn out,
Dancety, diddlety, poppety pin!

Before a Paisley baby could walk, his toes were tickled to this rhyme:

Feetikin, Feetikin, when will ye gang?
When the nichts are short an' the days are lang
I'll toddle an' gang,
I'll toddle an' gang!

'My grandfather in Alloa used to repeat this nonsense rhyme as he held one of us on his knee', says Elizabeth, 'depending on which member of the family he was dandling at the time, the bairn's name was inserted in the last line':

As I gaed ower the Brandy Hill
I met ma faither wi' guidwill,

> He had jewels, he had rings,
> He had many fine fine things;
> He had a cat wi' ten tails,
> He had a hammer wantin' nails;
> Up Jack! Doon Tam!
> Blaw the bellows for an auld man;
> The auld man has a cairrey coat
> Lying' in the ferry boat;
> The ferry boat is far owre dear,
> Ten pun' every year;
> Hauf a cherry, hauf a chess,
> Hauf a bonnie wee blue gless,
> Hauf a coo amang the corn
> Tae blaw oor little Geordie's horn!

There was a great deal of riding of horses in the old days, and a ride on father's foot or on his ever-ready knee was the happy substitute for a real 'powny'. The clicking and trotting sounds made during the ride were recognised by the baby long before he learned to speak.

A Kirkcaldy father would dandle his bairn on his knee while reciting:

> Cripple Dick upon a stick,
> Sandy on a soo,
> Ride a mile to Berwick, John,
> To buy a pun' o' 'oo.

A Perthshire mother sang:

> Ridin' on a horsie,
> Never standin' still,
> Doon by St Martin's an' ower by Newmill,
> In by Guildtown an' roon by Cargill,
> Richt by Burntbane an' ower by Gallowhill,
> Yont by the Harelaw an' doon tae Wolfhill
> An' *that's* the wey tae ride a horse
> An' never stand still!

My mother dandled us to this old rhyme:

> Hey diddle dumpling, my son John,
> Went to bed with his trousers on,
> One shoe off, and the other shoe on,
> Hey diddle dumpling, my son John.

Then she would toss us in the air, or part her knees letting us slip down the gap in her lap while we chortled with glee; or she would chant:

This is the way the ladies ride, jimpin' sma', jimpin' sma'
(gently bobbing up and down)
This is the way the gentlemen ride, trottin' an' a', trottin' an' a',

(jogging a little more actively)
But O! THIS is the way the cadgers ride, creels an' a', creels an' a'!
(bouncing us right off her knee and down again, several times in a most lively manner).

There are several versions of this enjoyable bit of fun; one goes:

This is the way the ladies ride, jimpity sma', fear gin she fa',
This is the way the gentlemen ride, trottin' an' a', trottin' an' a',
This is the way the cadgers ride, hobble–de–gee, creels an' a'!

The fun began with slow graceful riding like a lady, gradually degenerating into a boisterous ride like a cadger on a donkey.

And yet another version:

This is the way the ladies ride, trit, trot, trit, trot!
This is the way the gentlemen ride, gallop-a-gallopaway!
This is the way the farmers ride, hobble–de–dee, hobble–de–dee!
And DOWN into the ditch!   (falling between mother's knees)

Many a young father liked to dandle his baby boy on his knee, pretending that the child was a little horse to be taken to the farrier to get a new shoe. While reciting the rhyme he would take the child's foot and pat it firmly, first on the toe, then on the heel, then give him a bouncing ride. These were the words:

Jockie Smith, my fellow fine,
Can ye shoe this horse o' mine?

> Yes, indeed, an' that I can
> Jist as weel as ony man!
> Ca' a nail intae the tae,
> To gar the pownie clim' the brae!
> Ca' a nail intae the heel
> To gar the pownie trot weel!
> There's a nail an' there's a brod,
> An' there's a pownie weel shod,
>   weel shod, weel shod!
> A weel shod pownie!

Another hammering rhyme came from Dunfermline:

> Cobbler, cobbler, mend my shoe;
> I'll have it done by half-past two.
> Half past two is far too late,
> Have it done by half-past eight.

In the Shetland Isles, while dandling a baby, mothers sang:

> Dance, Dance, Dillifit,
> Sing, Aandren Young,
> Sheep's head up da taings
> An' du sall get da tongue!

(which meant 'there's a sheep's head roasting on the tongs and you shall have the tongue')
    Also:

> Baa, baa, baet dee
> Mammie's gaen ta sael dee,
> Fur ta pluck, an' fur ta pu'
> An' fur ta gadder lamb's 'oo,
> An' fur ta buy a bull's skin
> Ta row peerie-wearie in!

(This refers to the plucking of the wool of Shetland sheep which is done by hand.)
    And a few words, in passing, between a cat and a mouse:

> Da grey cat sat at da back door, spinnin',
> By cam' a peerie moose rinnin', rinnin':
> 'What's dis du's spinnin', my leddy, my leddy?'
> Cotton breeks ta me son, FAUSE TIEF, A'LL HAE DEE!

(Just as the cat is supposed to pounce on the mouse, a playful pounce was made on the baby!)

A similar conversation – this time between

The craa and the crab

Said the craa to the crab . . . 'Come a-shorrie, come a-shorrie!'
Said the crab to the craa . . . 'What furr? What furr?'
Again croaked the craa . . . 'Come a-shorrie, come a-shorrie!'
Replied the crab . . . 'A'm fairt at du rives me! A'm fairt at du rives me!'

(Croaking of the crow should be exaggerated to add to the effect.)

Stella remembers a Shetland mother holding a baby in her lap, with his two little legs in her hands, and crossing them, left over right and right over left, while chanting:

> Twa peerie penny dugs gaen tae da mill,
> *He* ower hims, an' *he* ower hims,
> Dat's da wy da peerie dug rins ta da mill;
> Dill, dill, dugs ta da mill,
> *Aff* a leg, an' *on* a leg, dill, dill, dill!

And here is the Fife version of this delightful bairn-rhyme: 'My grand-dad, with a baby boy on his knee, played with his little legs, crossing and re-crossing them while chanting:

> Leg ower, leg ower,
> Doggie ran tae Aberdour
> He cam' tae a stile
> An' UP he gaed ower!

(Lifting the child high, as over a stile, and placing him gently down as if on the other side).'

An elderly uncle in Dinnet recalled a rhyme in which the child is represented as a cogie in need of repairs. Counting the buttons on the little boy's coat, he recited:

> Donal' Cooper, Carle, quo' she,
> Can ye gird ma cogie?
> Couthie Carlin, that I can,
> As weel as ony bodie!

Then touching different parts of the child's body, he continued:

> There's ane aboot the mou' o't
> An' ane aboot the body o't,
> An' ane aboot the leggies o't,
> An' *that's* a girded cogie.

Andrew sang this rhyme to his small grand-daughter:

> Chubby Cheeks an' Paper Noddle
> Went out one day to catch a bogle,
> When the bogle did appear,
> Chubby Cheeks fell down wi' fear!

My mother would tickle a solemn baby under the chin and induce a chuckle from the most determined sobersides. With two fingers lightly 'walking' over the baby's head, she would gently touch, in turn, brow, eyes, nose, and mouth while telling the story:

> There was a wee man came over the hill,
> He knocked at the door,
> He keeked in,
> He lifted the latch
> And walked in!

or, as a variation, with the lightest of touch, she would repeat

> Broo broo brinkie,
> Eye eye winkie,
> Nose nose nebbie,
> Cheek cheek cherry,
> Mou' mou' merry,
> Chin chin chumpie,
> And BORE A HOLIE!
>> (chucking the baby under the chin)

I believe 'bore a holie' was my father's own addition; I have not heard of it in general use, but from Laurencekirk, his home-town, came a variant:

> Broo broo brinkie,
> Ee Ee winkie,
> Nose nose nebbie,

> Cheek cheek cherry,
> Mou' Mou' merry,
> Chin chin chackie,
> Catch a flea, catch a flea, curry
>   wurry, curry wurry.

(The last line is a chuckling accompaniment to a sustained tickling in the neck.)

From Freda, daughter of the owner of the famous Turra Coo, came another variation. Instead of *finishing* at the chin, she *began* the chant there, saying:

> Chin cherry,
> Mou' merry,
> Nose nappy,
> Ee winkie,
> Broo brinkie,
> An' awa' ower the hills tae Peterheed!

Another, starting at the chin and finishing at the top of the head, ran:

> Chin chin chackie,
> Mou' mou' merry,
> Nosie nosie nabbie,
> Cheek cheek cherry,
> Ee Ee winkie,
> Broo broo brentie,
> An' awa' ower the hill tae catch a rabbity!

From Turriff also came:

> Knock at the doorie,
> Keek in,
> Lift the sneck,
> Wipe yer feeties,
> An' walk in!

Marjory recalls a lovely bit of finger-play which never failed to delight a baby. All the fingers of one hand made a slow creeping movement from the baby's toes right up to his chest, and this is the story:

> There was a little moosie
> An' he couldna' get a hoosie,
> So he creepit up, an' creepit up . . . an' creepit up'
> Right up tae the littlin's bosie!

12

In many parts of Scotland they amused the baby by counting his tiny fingers. Beginning with the thumb they recited:

> This is the man that brak the barn,
> This is the man that stole the corn,
> This is the man that ran awa',
> This is the man that tellt a',
> An' puir wee pirly-winkie paid for a',
>   paid for a', paid for a'!

And the following well-known rhyme which crops up in many games was used:

> One, two, three, four, five,
> Can you catch a fish alive?
> Why did you let it go?
> Because it bit my finger so!

(Each finger in the baby's hand was held in turn, and when the pinkie was reached, it was given a tiny nip which was meant for the bite.)

In the same way they played with baby toes:

> This little pig went to market,
> This little pig stayed at home,
> This little pig got roast beef,
> This little pig got none,
> And this little pig cried 'Squeak, squeak,
>   squeak', all the way home!

From numerous sources have come rhymes for repetition when teaching a baby to clap his hands – for example:

> Clap handies all together,
> Clap clap away!
> This is the way we clap handies
> On Mammy's washin' day!

or:

> This is the way we clap handies
> On a rainy day!

and:

> Clap handies till Daddy comes hame
> For Daddy has siller an' Mammy has nane!

Also:

> Clap clap handies,
> Mammy's wee wean,
> Clap clap handies,
> Daddy's comin' hame;
> Hame 'til his laddie,
> Bonnie wee bit laddie,
> Clap clap handies,
> Mammy's wee wean!

A finger game which is still appreciated is:

Go round and round the garden like a Teddy Bear,
　　　　　(moving a finger round a baby's palm)
Go up one step　　　　(as far as the bend of his elbow)
Go up two steps　　　　(moving up to his shoulder)
(Then tickle him under the chin and make him laugh!)

While moving a finger round a little girl's palm, the old rhyme went:

> Lady, lady o' the lan'
> Can ye thole a kittly han'?
> If ye lauch or if ye smile
> Ye canna be a lady!

Jean remembers chuckling aloud when her grandfather regularly took her on his knee, and while running his fingers teasingly up from her wrist to her under-arm, and tickling her there, and all the way down her arm again, he would sing

> Adam and Eve went up my sleeve
> To buy a poke o' gundy,
> Adam and Eve came down my sleeve
> And said 'There's none till Monday!'

When I was old enough to sit on a swing my mother pushed, and chanted:

> Draw a bucket of water
> For my lady's daughter,
> One for a push
> Two for a push,
> Please, little lady, come into my hoose.

14

Another jingle to chant to a child on a swing went:

> Swingin' high an' swingin' low,
> This is the way the bairnies go,
> Doon tae the grun' an' up sae high,
> Jist like an aireyplane in the sky.

Agnes says that Shuggie was the name often given to a swing, and 'Gie's a shuggie' was the cry from bairns wanting a push. Nora heard her mother sing

> Shoo shuggie *doon* the glen
> Mammy's pet an' Daddy's hen.

which was Sutherland's preference. In other places they sang *up* the glen, or *ower* the glen.

In Aberdeen and Banffshire this was a favourite jingle with a gently swaying rhythm:

> Showdie, howdie, a pair o' new sheen,
> Up the Gallowgate, doon the Green.

The love of 'playing at horses' in most children began at the point when as babies they rode on their father's foot while he swung it to and fro to the chanting of the old nursery rhyme:

> Ride a cock horse to Banbury Cross
> To see a fine lady upon a white horse,
> With rings on her fingers and bells on her toes
> She shall have music wherever she goes!

Later, the child had a hobby-horse, one of the oldest of playthings, and if it did not strictly conform to the standard stick on two small wheels and a horse's head in wood, he made do with riding astride his father's walking-stick, trailing it along and leaving a most satisfactory furrow on a dusty road, while his mother strolled beside him singing:

> I had a little hobby-horse,
> His name was Dapple Gray,
> Its heid wis made o' pease-strae,
> Its tail wis made o' hay.
> I sold it tae an auld wife
> For a copper groat
> I winna sing a sang again
> Gin I win a braw new coat.

When my sister and I were very small we had home-knitted reins. The 'horse' thrust her arms through quoit-like rings, padded and covered with fabric, and attached to a breast-plate adorned with kitten-bells. The driver held the reins, long knitted strips, and the bells made a tinkling sound when the little horse trotted.

At Lumphanan Manse, where we often visited, there was a magnificent rocking-horse, pony-size, painted dapple-grey as were most rocking-horses, and rides on it were even better than the real thing. Mounted, we took the reins in our hands and at once, as if it were alive and not being zealously pushed by our hostess, the horse dipped forward and back, slowly at first, then faster and faster. Our hearts bursting with joy, we swayed in time with the horse. It was so exhilarating we could have kept it up for ever.

We were quite accustomed to getting a hurll in a farm-cart, jolting along to a dawdling clip-clop. Sometimes we were given a ride on the broad back of a cart-horse; the glossy hide moved with the horse, and it seemed to roll from side to side.

Cuddy is the Scots word for a donkey, but in the Lothians at one time it could also mean a horse.

When Lothian bairns played at horses, with reins they had made with a ball of rainbow wool, a pirn and four nails, they often sang:

> Hey, gae up, ma cuddy,
> Ma cuddy's ower the dyke,
> An' if ye touch ma cuddy,
> Ma cuddy'll gie ye a bite.

Falkirk bairns sang on the way to school:

> Twa Scotch horses gaun away tae Fife
> Comin' back on Monday wi' an auld wife.

Two girls skipped along side by side with their crossed hands joined. At the end of each couplet they changed places without breaking the hand-clasp, continuing to sing as they went along. In some places they sang:

> Twa Scotch horses gaun away tae Fife,
> Comin' back on Monday wi' a deid wife.

16

Another variant was:

> Trot, trot, horsie, gaun awa' tae Fife,
> Comin' back on Monday wi' a new wife.

And in Ayrshire it was:

> Scotch horses, Scotch horses,
> What time o' day?
> One o'clock, two o'clock,
> Three and away!

Auchterarder children played a game that Walter de la Mare is said to have quoted, and the rhyme went:

> I went to sea, no ship to get across,
> I paid ten shillings for an old blind horse,
> I sat on his back and was off in a crack,
> Sally, tell my mother I will never come back.

This is a song which Effie's mother used to sing to her in Gullane when she was very small. 'I loved it', she recalls, 'and remember bouncing up and down on my mother's knee. . . . I could not hear it too often.'

> Once upon a time there were three Jews.
> Once upon a time there were three Jews,
> Three-ee-ee Jews, Jews, Jews,
> Once upon a time there were three Jews.
>
> The first his name was Abraham,
> The first his name was Abraham,
> A-a-a-bra ham-ham-ham,
> The first his name was Abraham.
>
> The second his name was Isaac,
> The second his name was Isaac,
> Isa-sac-sac-sac,
> The second his name was Isaac.
>
> The third his name was Jacob,
> The third his name was Jacob,
> J-a-a cob-cob-cob,
> The third his name was Jacob.
>
> They all fell over a precipice,
> They all fell over a precipice,
> Preci-pice, pice-pice,
> And that was the end of these three Jews.

Bairns at Play

Charlie over the water
Charlie over the sea,
Charlie catch a blackbird
But can't catch ME!

Think now of little bairns at play.

'My little sister was always my special charge', mused a friend from Strathaven, 'and I can hear my mother's words ringing in my ears yet, when we went out to play "Noo, tak' care o' the littlin".'

'The street we lived in, in Kincardine-on-Forth', says Jean, 'was a lovely wide one, and not much traffic bothered us then. We had lovely summers in those days, and a high-light of our day was a visit from the man with the water-cart which sprayed jets of water to lay the stour. We used to run behind it in our bare feet. What fun it was! Sometimes a man with a barrel-organ brought a dancing-bear along, and we would dance and prance about with shouts of happy laughter.'

Bella remarks: 'Children do not have the peace and safety to play in the streets as our generation did. In our village square we played "Catties and doggies" by the light of gas-lamps and lighted windows . . . little children loved it. We joined hands and stood in a ring . . . Cattie stood inside, Doggie outside. They addressed each other:

"I am the doggie."
"I am the cattie."
"I can catch YOU!"
"No, you can't!"

Dancing bear

The dog then tried to get into the ring, and we tried to foil all his attempts, but we did all we could to help the cat by raising our hands to let him run out and in. When the cat was caught the dog took his place and a new doggie was chosen.'

'On frosty evenings in Perth', says Lindsay, 'between half-past four and six o'clock (we were not allowed out-of-doors any later) we played a sort of "I Spy" with a difference. The Spy had to stay in the dell (or den) till he heard a call from the others who were in hiding and sneaking from place to place. The call was a long-drawn-out cry, "Bae-ja-lum", but we never knew its meaning.'

When the bairns in Gourdon went off to hide one girl stayed behind, facing the wall with eyes closed, and counted to a hundred. Then she called, 'One, two three, I come' and went in search of the others. When she spied one she shouted, 'Treacle! Aw come oot!', and they had all to come out of hiding.

Emily remembers her childhood in Airdrie, then a small town with country roads and hedges only a few hundred yards from her home. 'The earliest game I remember', she says, 'was taught me by an elderly minister. Every time he came to call he would join hands with my little sister and me, and round we would all go, singing:

> I went to visit a friend one day,
> She only lived across the way,
> She said she couldn't come out to play
> Because it was her washing-day.

Then we would imitate all the actions of washing-day – we loved it!'

'Who's afraid of Black Peter', a much-loved game of young children, was, in Aberdeen, 'Who's afraid of the Big Black Beetle?'

One little boy stood at some distance with his back to the others, and called out, 'Who's afraid of the Big Black Beetle?', and they, creeping forward, replied 'No' me!' Again he called, 'Who's afraid?', and again they shouted 'No' me!', and drew a little nearer. When the Black Beetle thought they had come near enough he turned quickly and chased them.

In Glen Esk, for generations they played a game called 'Smuggle the Giggly', with its origin in smuggling days.

In Biggar, Burghead, and the tiny village (as it was then) of Skirling this game was called 'Smoogle', and the bairns shouted as they chased the 'smugglers', 'The Geg, the Geg, deliver up the Geg!' an obvious reference to the smuggling of kegs of spirituous liquor. The Geg, or Keg, was represented by any small article which could be concealed in the hand. Only the smugglers knew which of their number had the geg, and from the beginning of the game did their best to lure their pursuers away from him. When a smuggler was caught he was taken into custody, and if he had the geg he was ordered to hand it over and the other side became the smugglers, but if the geg-holder had been able to reach the den in safety his side won.

All down the ages little girls have loved to play at 'houses'. 'We loved keeping house with our own imaginary family', says Mary, 'and our game went on and on like a television saga. When we played at "schools" we were always very stern teachers, imposing strict discipline on our pupils, but I don't think we ever used the tawse.'

Few children can have had as their playtime 'house' a genuine Pictish broch. Before brochs were carefully preserved and placed under the protection of the National Trust of Scotland, Flora and her playmates used to play at houses in a Shetland broch. 'We were too young to know who the Picts were', she says, 'but we knew by the size of the broch that they were little people, and as we, too, were little people it was an ideal house for us, and we pretended to be Picts.' One little boy announced to a visitor, 'Ay, the Picts were here!', adding seriously, 'but they're no' here noo!'

Shetland children also played 'Farmyards', and filled them with a variety of animals of different sizes. These were contrived from the skulls of cows, sheep, and horses, and, for the smaller animals, cods' heads and lesser fish-bones. They attached string to the skulls and contentedly pulled their flocks and herds around.

'Flittin' da Kye' was one of their favourite ploys. Large cods' heads, after the family had dined off the fish, were purloined by the peerie lammies to use as kye. Each child had one, with a string attached for a tether, and a stake for the tethering. Each cow was jealously guarded and flitted, i.e.

staked at one spot after another, and woe betide any child whose cow invaded the territory of another.

'We loved playing housies and shoppies with only our imagination to furnish and equip them', said Emma, 'and we would search around for make–believe stuff to sell – sand was sugar, docken leaves were haddies, large round shilogie leaves were scones. We even had a housie game in which we joined hands in a ring singing to a girl in the middle:

> Who will come into ma wee hoose, ma wee hoose, ma wee hoose,
> Who will come into ma wee hoose, tae help me wi ma washin'!

The girl in the middle of the ring was expected to reply:

> O, I'll come into your wee hoose, your wee hoose, your wee hoose,
> O, I'll come into your wee hoose tae help you wi' your washin'.

but occasionally she would decide to reply:

> I'll *no'* come intae your wee hoose, your wee hoose, your wee hoose,
> I'll *no'* come intae your wee hoose, tae help you wi' your washin'!

in which case, all the girls would sing, with scorn:

> The dirty wee thing, she *wadna* come in, she *wadna* come in, she *wadna* come in,
> The dirty wee thing, she *wadna* come in, tae help me wi' ma washin'!

whereupon, instead of being invited to enter the wee hoose, as in the first case, she was slapped on the back, none too gently, by all the girls.

When bairns reached school age they were delighted to find that there were hosts of new games and ploys in which to take part. For example, there was 'Charlie over the Water'. Charlie was the bairn in the middle of the ring, and they all danced round him, singing:

> Charlie over the water
> Charlie over the sea,

Charlie catch a blackbird,
But can't catch ME!

When they sang the word ME each child stooped quickly and Charlie had to try to touch one of them before he could adopt a stooping position. The one he managed to tag took his place in the ring. There was 'Bobby Bingo', performed in a slow-moving ring:

Once a farmer had a dog,
His name was Bobby Bingo,
B-I-N-G-O, B-I-N-G-O, B-I-N-G-O,
His name was Bobby Bingo.

This was a singing game combined with counting-out to find the next bairn to go into the middle of the ring, and was sometimes sung as:

The farmer's dog's at our back door
And Bingo is his name-O,
B-I-N-G-O, B-I-N-G-O, B-I-N-G-O,
Bingo is his name-O!

In Dunfermline, little girls joined hands and moved round in a ring, singing:

Did you ever see a lassie, a lassie, a lassie,
Did you ever see a lassie do this way and that!

At this point the lassie in the middle gave a hop or a jump, did some fancy steps, or waved her arms, and the others stopped, dropped hands, and imitated her actions, while continuing to sing:

Do this way and that way, and this way and that way,
Did you ever see a lassie do this way and that?

In Auchterarder they sang:

When I was a lady, a lady, a lady,
When I was a lady, a lady was I.
It was this way and that way, and this way and that way,
And this way and that way, and this way went I!

The children acted the 'lady' by holding out their dresses and curtseying, and when the girl in the middle changed the word

23

to 'soldier', they marched round saluting. She chose a different person to imitate at every verse, and they copied her appropriate actions.

Little boys in Carluke often played 'Hoppy Currie', hopping about on one foot, with arms folded, and trying, by nudging, to knock each other off balance.

In Dundee they were fond of playing 'Blind Man's Buff', but *they* called it 'Jockie Blindie'.

'Fox, Hen and Chickens' was very exciting for little children. The Fox, an older child, faced the Hen, a bigger girl, who had all her little chicks behind her in a long line, each holding firmly to the waist of the one in front of her. The Fox tried hard to catch the little one at the end of the tail, while the Hen kept swaying the line from side to side to evade the Fox and protect her chicks.

Small children have always loved any ring game in which they all drop together to the ground. Such a game was

> Draw a bucket of water
> For my lady's daughter,
> Hush-a, hush-a,
> We all fall down.

For generations they have romped round, singing 'Ring-a-ring-a-roses' with no idea, fortunately, that the rhyme is said to date from the Great Plague of London, with its rose red spots and its sinister 'all fall down'. Very little ones liked this version,

> Ring-a-ring of roses,
> A pocketful of posies,
> A-tishoo, A-tishoo!
> (Imitating a sneeze, they all fell down.)

'When I first came to Glasgow from Yorkshire, at the age of six,' said Molly, 'I was used to singing:

> Ring-a-ring-a-roses, a pocketful of posies,
> Hush-a, hush-a, we all fall down;

but I soon had to change to the Glasgow version which was

> A ring-a ring-a roses, a cuppa-cuppa-shell,
> Ma man's awa' tae Hamilton tae buy a new bell,

If *ye* dinna tak' it, I'll tak' it tae masel
An' hide it in ma bosie, an' dinna you tell!'

Children love to be chased, and to give chase, and in Biggar they played every kind of 'Tig', including High Tig, Low Tig, and Chain Tig (or Copsy, probably derived from 'Cops and Robbers') which was a form of 'Hide-and-go-Seek', with commands like 'Lie low, Sheepie', 'Run, Sheepie, run', and 'Soom, Cuddy, soom'.

'I Spy' was another form of 'Hide-and-go-seek' which in Gullane was called 'Hessie'. One boy covered his eyes and counted to a hundred while the others scattered and hid. When he was ready to begin the search he shouted:

One, two, three,
Look out for me,
For I am comin'
An' I can see!

For each player he spotted he had to dash back to the den, hit the wall three times, and name the player he had spied. Any player could creep out and make a dash for the den, and if he reached it safely he went free.

In Glen Gairn we played this game every day throughout the summer. To us it was 'Tig-Dell-Free' (dell for den), running all over the moors, over by the pollocks, and up the hillside. When we wanted a moment's respite we would 'Cry a Barley', a corruption of the French 'Parlez' or parley, to indicate a pause.

There were numerous playground capers in which even the youngest child could take part – for example, two girls would grasp each other by the wrists, forming a seat on which they would carry a small girl around, to her great glee.

· Pick-a-back games are a survival of ancient tourneys. Big boys gave the small boys pickaback rides, which they called 'Collies'. Collie-back fights between two mounted boys were long ago very popular among school-boys.

A little boy would not have been long at school before he discovered the meaning of 'going halvers', giving a mate a half share. Whatever form of treasure there was to divide, the expected decision was 'We'll go halvers', but possibly not if he had already learned the Scots version of 'Findings keepings', which is, 'Nae bunchers, nae halvers, but a' ma ain!'

Clasping each other's hands, with arms crossed behind their backs, two girls would sometimes be seen skipping along, singing:

Jeanie Mac, Jeanie Mac, bonnie Jeanie MacGee,
Turn your back, turn your back, turn aboot tae me,
An' gin ye find, gin ye find, ony bawbee,
Pick it up, pick it up, an' gie it tae me!

In odd moments two boys might be seen seated on the ground, back to back, with their arms linked (or this could be done standing up). The aim was to lift the other boy off his feet, and the chant was

Weigh butter,
Weigh cheese,
Weigh a pun' o' can'le grease.

Swinging by a rope from a lamp-post was fun in the street, and could be at times adapted for the playground. 'There were pillars in our playground shed, where we sheltered when it rained', Elizabeth remembers, 'one girl would wind her arm round a pillar; another girl would cling to the free arm of the first and swing round.'

'Stookies', or 'Stues', got their name from stucco, from which plaster figures were made. 'Dinna stan' there like a stookie', was many an exasperated mother's cry to a reluctant child.

The game of 'Stookies' was played in a number of ways, but the basic rule was that the players must stand motionless, like statues, at the word 'Stop'. In Nithsdale they called it 'stookie dolls' and the winner was the one caught in the most amusing position.

A game for off moments was played by two girls facing each other, placing their fists alternately on top of the other's fists, piling them up in a column, by moving the bottom fist to the top, while chanting

One potato, two potato, three potato, four,
Five potato, six potato, seven potato, more.

and increasing the speed of the action until all was confusion.

In this ever-new finger-game two tiny wings of paper were

Weigh butter

placed on the nails of the forefingers resting on a table while the first two lines were recited. At the words, 'Flee awa', a flying motion over the shoulder was made, and the *middle* finger brought back, mystifying the child. At the words, 'Come back', the flying motion was repeated, and miraculously Peter and Paul reappeared.

The Scots rhyme for this little teaser was:

> Twa little dicky-birds sat upon a wa',
> Ane wis ca'd Peter, the tither ca'd Paul,
> Flee awa', Peter, flee awa' Paul,
> Come back, Peter, come back, Paul.

Other finger games come to mind.

For 'The Baby's Cradle' the words were

> Here's the lady's forks and knives
> (palms uppermost, fingers interlaced and
> pointing upwards)

27

Here's the lady's table
  (turn hands over to show the backs,
    making a fine table)
Here's the lady's looking-glass
  (raise the thumbs to form a peak)
And here's the baby's cradle.
(Raise the little fingers as well, making the two ends of the cradle. Then rock the cradle, rock, rock, rock, backwards and forwards, *never* sideways, lest the baby fall out of the cradle.)

'Grannie taught me this one', says Elspeth:

This is the church,
This is the steeple,
These are the doors
And these are the people.
Here is the preacher going upstairs
    (some say the 'pope' or the 'parson')
And here in the pulpit he's saying his prayers.

Fingers interlaced inside the hands represented the people in church; thumbs pointing upwards side by side formed the doors; forefingers pointing upwards touching each other's tips made the steeple. We then opened the doors and turned the hands over to show the people. In the next action we hooked the pinkie of the right hand over the pinkie of the left, then the next finger over the same finger of the left hand, continuing till all were locked. Done neatly and swiftly this represented the preacher going upstairs. Then we turned the hands till the thumb of the left hand was poking through the circle made by the right hand, and that represented the preacher in the pulpit.'

Incy Wincy Spider climbed up the water-spout,
Down came the rain and washed poor Incy out;
Out came the sun and dried up all the rain,
Incy Wincy Spider climbed the spout again.

This old finger-game was very popular among little girls. Touching the first finger of the left hand to the thumb of the right, circling them alternately with the first finger of the right hand and the thumb of the left, in a continuous movement they continued the play as if climbing the water-spout.

They wiggled all the fingers to indicate falling rain, and turned their palms downward and moved them from side to side to indicate the washing out of Incy. Palms were then turned upward, and slowly raised to indicate the coming out of the sun. The climbing action was then repeated. This was neat and quick, and children never wearied of doing it at odd moments.

A vulgar parody appealed to teasing boys. . . .

> There was a bloomin' sparra climbed up the bloomin'
>   spout,
> An' then the bloomin' rain came an' washed the
>   sparra out,
> Then the bloomin' sun came out an' dried the
>   bloomin' rain,
> Then the bloomin' sparra went up the spout again.

Another parody concerned a motor car:

> Eency Weency Minnie went up the road to town,
> Down came the rain and washed the Minnie
>   down,
> Out came the sunshine and dried up all the rain,
> But Eency Weency Minnie was never seen again.

A modern finger-game was supplied by one of my grandchildren, and the words are:

> A houlet and a heron,
> A pyot and a kae,
> Cam' tae First Fit me
> Aince upon a day.
> The houlet juist gowped,
> The kae gie'd me gab,
> The pyot ryped my poke,
> And the heron played . . . DAB!

In guessing games it was usual to recite:

> Nievie, nievie, nick, nack
> Which han' will ye tak'?
> Tak' the richt or tak' the wrang,
> I'll beguile ye if I can.

29

A Border version was:

> Nievie, Nievie, nick, nack
> Which han' will ye tak',
> Tak' the teen an' leave the tither
> For the auld gran' mither.

That was the boys' favourite – the girls had another. 'In Forfar', says Bessie, 'all the girls could take part; they stood in a row with extended fists. One stood aside. She was the one who had to do the guessing. Another was chosen to be the Queen of Sheba. They all chanted:

> The Queen of Sheba has lost her gold ring,
> Lost her gold ring, lost her gold ring,
> The Queen of Sheba has lost her gold ring,
> Guess who has found it!

'The Queen of Sheba went along the line touching each girl's hands. Into one she placed the ring, and the one who was "out" had to guess where it was hidden. If correct, the finder became the Queen, but if wrong, she had to be "out" again.' Riddles have always been popular, and the old, old favourites are still to the fore – for example:

> A wee, wee hoosie, fu' fu' o' meat
> Wi' neither door nor window
> To get in to eat.   (An egg)

and

> A wee, wee man
> Wi' a red, red coat
> A staff in his hand
> And a stone in his throat,
>   Come a-riddle, come a-riddle
>   Come a-rote, tote, tote.   (A cherry)

and

> Little Nancy Etticoat
> In her white petticoat,
> The longer she stands,
> The faster she goes.   (A lighted candle)

And all those schoolboy 'catches', for example:

Constantinople is a very hard word to spell . . . can you spell it?   (IT)

'During my first year at school', says Effie, 'a teacher taught us a singing game in class which we found pleasantly terrifying. One child, representing a mother, sat singing to her baby:

> Hush ye, hush ye, little pet ye,
> Hush ye, hush ye, do not fret ye,
> The Black Douglas shall not get ye.

'At this point a boy representing the Black Douglas appeared behind the Mother, gripping her by the shoulder and saying grimly, "I'm not so sure about that" – whereupon the Mother swooned!'

This was founded on a story that used to be told about the recapture of Roxburgh Castle. Douglas, leading his men by twos and threes, crept silently through the dusk and effected an entrance. The first person he encountered was a woman singing her child to sleep. Suddenly, as she sang 'The Black Douglas sall not get ye', a steel-gloved hand was laid on her arm and a voice said, 'I'm not so sure of that!' It was the Black Douglas himself!

Jessie recalls a charming game that little boys and girls played in Nether Dallochy. It was called 'Hawkie, Hawkie'.

A Hawk was chosen and had to count slowly up to twenty with his face hidden and eyes shut. The other children scattered in all directions. Each one pulled some grass and fashioned a nest, then, finding a secret hiding-place, put the nest in it and one or two small stones inside it for eggs, then ran back to the Hawk shouting, 'Hawkie, Hawkie, harry my nest.' He then had to set out to find and scatter the hidden nests.

Elsie has recalled David Wingate's verses on the finicky, peevish child, described by him as

The Dorty Bairn

> Preserve me, Lizzie Allan,
> Hae ye no' your breakfast taen?
> Sic a face ye hae wi' greetin'!
> What's the matter wi' ye, wean?

Ay! a flee ran ower your parritch?
Fanny snowkit at your breid?
My certie! Leddie Lizzie,
Ye're a dainty dame indeed!

But the parritch can be keepit,
An' the breid can be laid by;
An' if hunger proves nae kitchen
Then the tawse we'll hae to try.

Ay! a bairn may weel be saucy
When there's plenty an' to spare;
But there's mony a better lassie
Wad be blythe tae see sic fare.

Oh, Lizzie, Lizzie Allan!
Ye maun mend, or ye shall learn
That it's mair o' cuffs than cuddlin'
That awaits a dorty bairn!

Games in the Street

Me an' ma Grannie an' a hale lot mair,
Kickit up a row on the wash-house stair,
By cam' a bobby an' cried 'Wha's there?'
'Jist me an' ma Grannie an' a hale lot mair.'

The study of children's games, however superficial, reveals that they are a great deal more interesting than those of adults which they frequently copy, and imitation, which covers a vast spectrum of life, is a basic way in which a child develops.

Modern civilisation with its high-rise flats, high-density housing and traffic problems, interferes greatly with the spontaneous play of children.

Heavy traffic is mainly to blame for putting an end to many old street games, but so is the demolishing, in cities, of tenements with their communal backyards full of wash-houses and other out-houses where children could safely play. They had their closes, too, to play in, and the whitewashed walls bore evidence of many a battle with a headered ba'. Houses now being closed in, children cannot play 'Kick the Can' at the back door any more.

'We played "Kick the Can" in the streets of St Andrews in cold weather', says Euphie, 'any can with its bottom and lid knocked out would do. The game was started by kicking the can along the cobbled streets. You can imagine the noise, especially if you remember that, at that time, most boys wore tackety boots. The game was not very popular with our elders and betters, as the phrase goes.' 'Kick the Can' was called 'White Hankie' in Glasgow.

Mina recollects that it was a favourite game in Midlothian. 'We enjoyed it', she says, 'because both big and little children could play it together, and we little ones were proud to be picked for one of the sides. After the can had been kicked, and while it was being fetched back to the den, we went to ground up the closes and down by the burn-side. The one who was Het had to search for us and bring us in. Meanwhile, a clever player could creep up and, with a triumphant cry of "Kick the Can", send it spinning away again, and set the captives free.'

Robert remembers that the can was usually a syrup or treacle tin and the selected hider would kick it as far as he could down the street from the base. The seeker had to run as fast as he could to recover the can and replace it at the base, during which time the hiders were out of sight. The further the can was kicked, the longer it took the seeker to recover it and the longer the hiders had in which to find hiding-places. There were generally plenty of places – up 'outside stairs', or down back-stairs and in back-greens, so the seeker had a difficult task. If he appeared to be making little progress the hiders would shout (giving him a clue to their whereabouts):

> Come oot o' yer den, ye dirty hen,
> An' look for a' yer chickens.

Meg recalls lively kick-the-can parties in a spacious stable-yard at Broughton, and also skilful games of bicycle-polo, a favourite ploy of her older brother and sister.

'"Throw the Lamp" was similar to "Kick the Can" except that we did not have to throw a lamp', says Robert. The seeker had to stand close to a lamp-post, facing it with his eyes shut, and count up to twenty fairly slowly to give the others time to hide.

Communal games were exciting when played by children of all ages and both sexes. 'We played "Kick the Can" in this way in Dunfermline', says Betty, 'with teams chosen by a counting-out method. At the beginning of the game we cried, "The Can's away!"'

Harry points out that it was understood in Edinburgh games in 1910-13 that one did not hide anywhere more than fifty yards from the den.

At Gourdon, it was the leader who first kicked the can,

shouting 'Aw' come oot!' They all came out and the can was kicked from one player to another, each endeavouring to return it to its starting-point. The player who achieved this, having put his foot on the can and shouted 'Block the Can', became the leader.

'We played "Block the Can" in the stackyard at our Aberdeenshire farm', says Mabel, 'a game in which everybody took part, and which our fathers, and their fathers, had played before us.'

George regrets that 'children can no longer play, as we did, on our High Street, and in its closes, wynds, and back-yards. What a glorious place it was for a monster game of rounders, cat-and-bat, lamp-post tig, and a game with the very odd name of "Saut"! We played with a screaming intensity now reserved for the appearance of pop stars.

'I recall a terrific game called "Hoist the Flag", probably based on a folk-tale relating to the relief of a besieged castle. Any number could play. One side remained in the den, which was usually a shop-door or a close. The other side went and hid. When they were set, one of their number returned and in dumb show gave directions to the hide-out. No cheating or misleading was allowed; it was up to the hunters to interpret the signs and try to find their quarry. If they found them there was a wild race to the den, and whoever reached it first yelled "Hoist the Flag!" but if the hunters went hopelessly astray, the one who had given the directions signalled to the hidden side, and they made a concerted rush to the den.'

It was known as 'Hoist the Flaggie' in Brechin, and in St Andrews, where they played round the street-lamps after dark.

The game of 'Release' or 'Relieve', also had the theme of fugitives and captors, and for hundreds of years was known all over Scotland under different names, the rules being basically the same.

It was a summer game in Crathie, according to Alice. 'Prisoners were put in a den with a guard. If one of the IN side could get close enough to dart between prisoner and guard, he shouted "Release!" and the prisoner was free to rejoin his side. It was *most* exciting if all but one of the IN side had been caught, and if that one, by skill and cunning, was able to release all the

members of his side that *was* a triumph! When all were taken
we changed sides. We never seemed to tire of this game, and,
when played at home, our parents had quite a time calling us in
at bedtime!'

In Falkland they called it 'Lievo', an abbreviation of
'Relieve-O'. Euphie says an unlimited number of boys and
girls could join in. One team stood in the den, the others
scattered in all directions. 'We *did* set boundaries', she says, 'so
that the Lomond Hills did not have to be scoured! Once the
team in the den had counted slowly to ten with eyes closed
they set off in twos and threes in search of the others. A touch
was sufficient for a capture.'

In Langholm, however, captives were permitted to struggle
to get free while their captor counted to ten; after that, they
had to submit.

Colin recalls that in Annan the game was played on strategic
lines with pursuers working in pairs to cut off the 'slow-
coaches' on the other side, and the pursued bunching and
splitting up, sending one fast runner to draw off the guard, and
another to run through the den while the guard was
temporarily engaged, shouting a triumphant 'Lee-voy-Oot!'
Lee-voy was a childish corruption of 'Relieve-O', which in
some places became 'Levoy' and 'Leavey'.

'A-lee-voy', 'Hall-lee-voy', 'Hallie-leevey', were other
variants of the name in use in different districts of Edinburgh.

'We played "Relievers" in George Square in Edinburgh,
which I left in 1917. It was especially thrilling on darkish
afternoons in Colinton', Jem remembers, 'and guaranteed to
keep us out-of-doors a good deal later than approved by our
parents.'

In Leith the game was 'Leroy', understood to be a
corruption of 'Relieve all'.

'We played it in the streets of Edinburgh in 1910-1915. A
den about six feet square was chalked against a wall or corner,'
Jack remembers. 'Our den had to have two solid sides and two
open ones, generally a corner formed by a building. The
patrolling guard had to keep one foot inside and one outside
the den. If at any time he was spied with both feet inside or
both out, captives could rush out and get away. If a fugitive
could outwit his pursuers and reach the den, he would try to

put one foot inside and shout "A-lee-voy!" Then all the captives regained their freedom. This took some ingenuity but was quite often successful.'

'We usually played it in the winter-time in our small seaside village,' says Ellie. 'There were no street-lights then, only that of the moon and the stars. The village is now well-lit, but there are not so many open spaces and places for children to hide in. It was the prisoners, in our game, who gave a long-drawn-out cry of "Relieve-O-O-O!" to attract the attention of their side, and bring them to their rescue.'

'Stocky Out' and 'Stocky In' were cries in another version of the game.

'We played "Relieve-oy" in a large square with a garden in the centre', Dee remembers, 'with a street coming in at each corner, and numerous doorways in which to hide. What with these *and* the garden, our pursuers had their work cut out to find us.'

'When I was a pupil at James Gillespie's High School for Girls in Edinburgh', says Lilias, 'we played "Levoy", not in the street, but in the school grounds. Our den backed on to the school wall in a nice open space. One team went off, not necessarily to hide, but to dash tantalisingly around, while the others tried to catch them by tigging. The captives were put in a den guarded by several girls, because the only way to free them was for one of their side to creep up and get a foot in the den, at the same time shouting "Levoy"! We played the game day after day, starting at the point where we left off the previous day. Girls who went home to lunch hurried back to join in. This was a glorious opportunity to rescue prisoners, if you could get in before your opponents were aware of your return! As we grew older we speculated on the meaning of the word, "Levoy". Some of us felt it must have some relationship to the French "lever", to raise, as in raising a siege . . . others thought we were shouting "Relieve all".'

Janet recalls that little girls in Leith in the 1920s played a game which they called 'Alla-lee-voy', hopping on one foot with arms folded, which in other districts of Scotland was known as 'Hoppy Currie'.

Mary calls to mind 'a game we played in our street with great fervour during the long summer evenings. It was called

"Stand Fire" and was played by two teams of equal size, A and B, facing each other about twenty yards apart. A player in A threw a ball to B. If it was caught the whole team had to stand like stookies while the catcher in B aimed the ball at the legs of a team-member in A. This was a great opportunity to capture the team's most accurate thrower, as, if she was touched by the ball below the knee, she had to change sides. If she was untouched the ball was thrown again by A. In the end, the team which acquired the most players was the winner. In those days nobody in our street owned a car, and passing cars were as few as passing policemen, so our game was uninterrupted for long periods. Mums used to come to their doors to watch us at play and to have a chat.'

In 'Crossing the Water', as played in Airdrie, according to James, a selected small squad of boys stood in the centre of the village square, their object being to arrest those who were not fleet-footed enough to break through the resistance line. It was much the same in Tarves – crossing continued till the boys in the middle by far outnumbered those who dashed across from one side to the other. The game ended only when no free runners were left.

There were endless games that involved crossing the street from one side to the other. Such a game was called, in Dunfermline, 'Tigmanarty'. The girl who was Het stood at one side of the road facing a wall, with her hands clasped behind her back. The other girls moved very quietly from the other side of the road, their object being to cross over and touch her hands. Should she turn round, which she was entitled to do at any time, and saw someone moving, that girl had to take her place.

In 'Bar the Door', a single player was dared to cross alone. The others stood and watched while he tried to 'jouk' past the boy in the middle of the road who had called him out. If he succeeded in crossing he cried 'Bar the Door' and they all rushed across in a body. In some places the shout was 'Bar the Window', or 'Bar the Keyhole'. Border bairns called it 'Joukie' because they had to jouk past the one in the middle. In Aberdeen it was known as 'Burrie', and it was still being played in Forfar in 1910.

In Leith, 'Stookies' was a game that involved crossing. Jane

38

'Bar the Door'

says: 'The one who was Het could turn round suddenly while you were trying to cross the road. If she caught you moving you had to freeze in your tracks like stookies, and everything possible would be done to induce you to move.'

Every traditional game is subject to radical and sometimes rapid changes, e.g. 'Charlie, Charlie, may I cross the water' in the distant past was a reference to Bonnie Prince Charlie. A revised version became 'Charlie Chaplin, may I cross the water?', which, in its turn, probably became obsolete. In the game, one person asked the question; the others stood ready to cross. When permission was given to cross, there was the usual mad rush.

'In Dumfries', says Roy, 'we played "Keehoy" with great regularity. All the boys lined up on one side of the square, having selected one of their number to stand in the centre, and he had the privilege of calling on one, or more, by name, or all of us, to "cross over". If he succeeded in catching anyone that boy had to stay with him and help in the catching. This went on till the last boy was caught.'

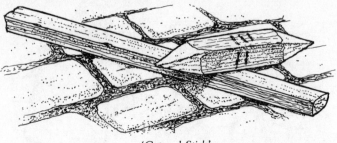

'Cat and Stick'

'Change a Pound' was a game played in Fife about 1886. Several players took part, each standing in a den, in a ring. One stood in the middle. The idea was that if A wanted to change a pound with D or F they quickly changed places and the one in the middle tried to reach a vacant den. The odd man out had to go in the middle.

'Many years ago, in Elgin', says Nigel, 'we would scrape up a small heap of earth, and all go dancing round it in a ring, pulling and pushing each other with the object of forcing someone to step on the heap. No penalty was exacted, but those caught in the act suffered a momentary loss of face. The game was simple enough but I have at times wondered at the ancient implications of the game . . . "Burn the Bible". I have heard of a ploy in which a boy elected to stand on a street-grating shouting "Burn the Bible" till he was pushed off his so-called castle, and another boy became "king".'

David remembers in his early youth being involved in the building of actual bonfires. 'We danced round them in a ring, and tried to push one another into the flames.'

Robert recollects that the game of 'Cat and Stick' was played with a bat or stick and a small piece of wood, four to six inches long, sharpened at both ends, and numbered on its four flat sides in Roman numerals. A variety of games was played with this simple equipment, all on the principle of hitting the 'cat' with the stick while it was in the air.

One version was called 'Tip Cat' or 'Waggles'. Four boys stood at the corner of a square; two had bats, the others were feeders and threw up the 'cat'. The batsman hit the cat as far as possible, and, when the feeder was retrieving it, seized runs for his side. If either cat fell to the ground, both batsmen were OUT, and the feeders had their turn.

Alice mentions that it was called 'Stick and Guinea' in Hawick in 1900, and Saul informs us that in Newton Mearns, and in Falkirk, the game was called 'Cat and Bat'. 'We borrowed Mother's hat-pin', he recalls, 'and made the point red-hot in the fire. Then we burned the numerals into the wood of the "cat", which we hit on one end with a small cricket-bat. It flew into the air, and in its flight we hit it again and again, swiping it as far as we could. When it settled on the ground the number seen to be uppermost was noted and these were added together after three hits, or rather, when the cat was grounded three times. The highest total proclaimed the winner. We used to play in the street but were foiled by the advent of the motor-car.'

According to Doreen, "Catty and Batty" was played by Burghead girls in Spring and Summer, either by two people or as a team game. The bat was just a stickie shaped at one end to make a gripping handle. Our fathers and brothers shaped stickies and a catty for our use, burning on the numerals with a red-hot poker. With a shoe-heel we made a hole in the soft earth, or on the sea-shore. First, the stickie was placed across the hole and the leader of the opposing side threw the catty at it. Next, the catty was set in the hole with a point showing, and when it was hit, it became airborne, and could then be walloped as far from the hole as possible. The number of strikes depended on which numbers on the catty were showing. The score was arrived at by measuring the distance from the hole in bat-lengths, turning it over and over from the point where the catty had landed.' In Sprouston, near Kelso, a similar game was known as 'Sticky'.

' "Catty and Batty" was played in Dundee', says Norman, 'the catty being fashioned from an odd piece of wood whittled with a pocket-knife. The batty, more often than not, was a spar from a condensed-milk box. The non-batting team scattered around to be ready to catch the catty when it was struck by the batsman. This he did by holding it aloft in one hand, while with the bat in the other he belted it out among the fielders. If the catty was caught he was dismissed, and the next member of his side took over. There were numerous

Bools

intricacies in the game; the rules could vary from street to street.'

Margaret recalls a simplified game of 'Cat and Bat' for one or more players which was played in Crathie. Each player used a bat-shaped piece of wood, and the object was to keep a small pebble aloft for as long as possible without its touching the ground.

Marbles, so called because away back in the fifteenth century or so, they were originally made of marble, have always been known as 'bools' in Scotland, from the French, 'Boule'. A healthy loon was never at a loss for amusement so long as he carried half-a-dozen bools in his pocket. A game could be arranged at any time, provided that another boy had some bools and agreed that a game was 'on'.

'In our glen the loons played at bools in the Spring', says Stewart, 'when the days were lengthening. They made in the soft earth a hole in which their bools were placed; then, one by one, they would span the ground with grubby paws, and flick the bool expertly between the knuckles of a bent thumb and

42

curved forefinger, suddenly straightening the thumb to make the shot that would knock out his opponents' bools. Ten a penny in the 1900s, they were made of baked clay, glazed brown or oatmeal-colour, and were called by different names . . . "commonies" (the least valuable), "alleys" (the most valuable, reserved for use as "taws") and "stonies". There were also treasured glass ones with streaks of bright colours through them, which were called "glessies", and greatly prized.' I have been told a true story of a laddie in Aberuthven, with his head and his pocket full of bools; when, in class, the teacher asked him 'what is the female of bull?' he pondered, then hesitatingly suggested, 'A glessie?'

Lemonade bottles were sealed with a green glass marble inside the neck, which you pressed down with your thumb to open. Break the neck of an empty bottle and you got a green glessie for naethin'!

Jean explains that a taw was the biggish bool actually used by a player from his stance approximately six feet away. His opponent would, in Kincardine-on-Forth, have insisted that he 'knuckle down to it', meaning that the knuckle of his forefinger must be touching the ground; when he flicked his thumb and scored a hit a triumphant yell would go up. This happened at every good shot.

Lindsay recalls that 'In March and April bools were the order of the day in Perth. Our favourite games were "ringie", "puddley scories", and "moshey". Ringie required a circle about five inches across into which we each placed four bools. We each had a "plunker", i.e. a "chuckie", a "glessie", or a "goldie". We plunked, holding the bool between finger and thumb, from the edge of the circle. Throwing was taboo. For each bool that you shot out of the ring you were allowed another "go".'

'Our favourite game of bools was called "Spanny",' says George, 'and the best spot in our High Street for it was right in front of our house. From the pavement the ground sloped slightly, and was bumpy with moss and hidden stones. Stooping, the first player gently struck his bool against the edge of the pavement. It zig-zagged down the slope, coming to rest at some unpredictable spot in the ditch. The next player repeated the performance, hoping to place his bool as near as possible to the first. If by chance he hit it, that was a clear win; if the two bools lay within the span of our outstretched fingers, and the thumb and pinkie could flick them together, that was also a win – hence the name – spanny. But if he failed to score, the third player attempted to get his bool within the span of the others . . . so the game went on – a nice, quiet, placid game, you would say? but like many of our pastimes, it frequently ended in a brawl!'

A similar game mentioned by Robert was played along the gutter. The first player would knuckle his bool along a clean dry gutter; the next player would do the same, trying to hit the first player's bool. The third and other players would follow suit. The first player would then knuckle his bool further along the gutter (if not already hit and taken) in which case he would have to replace it from his stock of bools. The other players followed, knuckling their bools from the spot where they had come to rest. Quite long distances could be covered in this game. The bools, of course, had to be lifted over 'sivers', which were water drains in the gutter.

Girls in Arbroath carried their bools in little cotton bags. Red clay bools called 'dods' were their favourites, and, of course, the expensive and highly-prized glessies.

I once heard of a man who made and sold bools of inferior clay which disintegrated during play, because they were only half-baked. It was a mean trick to play on trusting children.

The game of 'Nicking' was played with seven or eight buttons, usually 'sinkeys' which were the metal or brass buttons commonly used on trousers. They had a slight depression (hence the name) and four holes through which strong thread was passed. 'Shankeys' were the kind sewn on with a shank or loop. Even as far back as 1892, it seems, trouser buttons were hard to come by; boys were driven to cutting them off their own breeks, replacing them before their mums found out.

In Fife, a circle was drawn on the ground, and a button placed in the centre. The players stood at a distance, and each in turn threw a button into the circle. The player whose button landed nearest the one in the centre was allowed to pick up as many buttons as he could by pressing them with his thumb-nail.

In another version of the game, trial shots were played to decide who should go in first. Each in turn stood on the kerb, and took his 'nicker' (a piece of lead melted and flattened) and aimed it at the target. If he hit it, he got that button and another go. If he missed, another boy went in. The winner was the boy who collected the most buttons.

'Pitch and Toss' was strictly forbidden, but boys in towns sometimes risked a game, as the following rhyme discloses:

> At the Cross, at the Cross,
> Where we played 'Pitch and Toss',
> And the bobby cam' an' chased us away,
> We ran and we ran an' we fell ower a man,
> An' that wis the end o' oor play.

Jim says 'Dundee laddies gambled with buttons, which were given different values. "Twecks" were rated according to size and ornamentation; "mites" were small and rated merely one point. Players had to pitch their buttons to land on a certain target; those who succeeded were allowed to "kill" (annex) the buttons of those who missed.'

'Pinner' was a game played with heavy metal objects, and, though extremely popular among older boys, was a menace to the younger ones who were apt to get in the way.

The ancient game of 'Chuckie Stanes', 'Chuckies' or 'Checkers' was played all over the country, sometimes with ten stones, more frequently with five. In villages on the Ayrshire coast, five pebbles were used. One was thrown in the air, and one of the others, arranged in a square on the ground, had to be picked up before the first one came down and was caught. Then two at a time were thrown up, then three, and four. A variant was to toss the chuckies from the back of the hand, while chanting

> My little puppy-dog
> Likes sweet milk.

Five small smooth stones plus one bool were used in Aberdeen. They were placed in a circle on the pavement. Each girl knelt in turn, threw the bool into the air, and picked up one stone before the bool came down. While she proceeded to

45

pick up two, three, four, and five stones, she chanted, making sweeping movements with her hand. . . .

> Sweep the flairie,
> Lift the chairie,
> Sweep ablow it,
> Lay it doon.

A ball to stot, instead of a bool to throw, was used in some districts, and two, three and four chairs were lifted, as in the rhyme above, till all the chuckies had been replaced.

The method of playing Chuckies in Edinburgh and Fife, Sheila describes. This was to place five small stones in the palm of the hand, then throw them in the air, saying 'Five'. The hand was then turned so that the stones, descending, fell on the back of the hand. This was repeated seven times, counting, 'ten, fifteen, twenty, twenty-five, thirty', up to forty-five.

There were many other ways of using Chuckie Stanes (and some very complicated variations) but one was simplicity itself.

This was for two wee boys, who would each collect ten little stanes about the size of a pea. One boy put his hands behind his back and manoeuvred, say, four of his stanes into his right hand, which he then brought forward and asked, 'How many stanes are in my hand?' If the other boy guessed correctly he was given the four stanes. If he guessed wrong and said 'five' he had to hand over a stane, having guessed one too many. If he guessed 'two' he had to hand over two, having guessed two too few. In every case the difference on either side of the actual number had to be paid. The object was to win ten stanes and end up with twenty.

' "Scotch or Irish" was a seasonal occurrence but I don't remember in which season it occurred', says Robert. 'It lasted for a few weeks each year. Each boy would prepare a large paper-ball tied with string, leaving a couple of yards of string by which to hold it. They then went around the streets shouting "Scotch or Irish", quizzing the boys they met, and if one answered "Irish", the paper ball was sent whirling in a menacing fashion round his head. The balls were soft and no injury was normally done, but rougher elements from a different locality from the boys who ordinarily played this game, would sometimes join in and wrap a stone inside a paper ball, so that it became quite an offensive weapon. I don't remember ever hearing a boy actually reply "Irish" (we were all Scots!) but we liked to walk about swinging these paper balls round our heads, and shouting "Scotch or Irish"!'

James from his home in California, has called to mind some of the games he played long ago with his pals in the Maryhill and Cowcaddens areas of Glasgow. A naturalised American citizen for many years he can still recall 'Fit an' a hauf', where one boy was picked to be the 'doon', and placing his heels against the kerb, bent over while the others leap-frogged over his back into the roadway. When the last boy had leaped, the 'doon' moved forward and took up a new position on the spot where the last boy had landed. The boys then repeated the leap-frogging, still from the kerbside. Each time the 'doon' moved forward, so that clearing his back became more difficult – the first boy who failed to clear, or who required a step into the roadway, became the next 'doon'.

Hop Scotch, or Scotch Hoppers, got its name because the child who was trying to get the peever into a square could only hop over the lines which were scotched, that is, traced on the pavement. It was never called by that name in Scotland. As Peevers it was popular among both boys and girls, and was the universal game played by girls practically the whole year round. It was essentially a pavement game because the lines between the flagstones made natural 'beds', and a hard, smooth surface was best for the shuffling, or scliffing, of the peever, which, along with a piece of chalk, was all that was required for the game. As soon as the first fine days of Spring arrived, out came the chalk to mark out the beds in squares and rectangles. If the beds were long, resting-places were provided.

Peevers were called 'pallies' or 'pallallies' in Angus; they were 'pauldies' in St Andrews and 'boxes' in Aberdeen.

The game consisted of hopping and kicking a round marbly stone from bed to bed, starting all over again if at any time it rested on a line. This was the basic rule, but the beds could be laid out in simple or in very complicated designs, with the initials of those taking part inscribed on the beds. When enough players had been enrolled, as it were, it was customary

Peevers

to display a notice which read, 'No more to play . . . so don't
ask'.

'Our peever was a round flat stone about two inches in
diameter and not quite an inch thick, though size did not
matter', Jen remembers. 'I believe they were made from pieces
of stone left over from the stone-masons' yards, and were sold
in the wee sweetie shops and hardware stores. They were
slightly polished which made them slippy, and from much use
they got slippier. If you couldn't afford to buy one for a penny
or tuppence, a piece of broken tile or earthenware would do,
or a shoe-polish tin filled with earth. When the tin was first
thrown in you had to hop to the top and back again, skipping
the tin along with your feet. You continued like this till you
had been in every numbered bed, but if you touched a line you
were OUT.' The only variation to the practice of sliding the
peever along the ground was to place it on the raised foot while
hopping. This was known as 'carrying the baby to London'.

'In Fife', says Ann, 'we played peevers with a flat stone or
block, which we moved from bed to bed avoiding the lines.

48

First, the block was moved to a chant of "Onesie, twosie, threesie, tossie, bossie"; next it was "Hen scrape" (moving the block and giving two scrapes with the foot); then came "Crack a Bake" (after moving the block, putting down heel and toe); after that came "Pigs' feet" (moving the block with both feet together); followed by "Double pigs' feet" (jumping with both feet over the lines after moving the block); finishing with "Blue bottle" (moving the block right round the beds, while holding your left foot behind your back with your right hand.'

Margaret remembers that as a child in Edinburgh in the 1920s, one of the most popular games, especially for girls, was peevers. 'Stones could be bought for a few pence and I still have one I bought over forty years ago!'

'Prally boxes' was another name for peevers. 'The prally', says Anne, 'was either a flat round tin, or a broken bobbin-head from the spinning-shed in a factory. Girls became very expert at hopping the prally from one bed to the next without fouling the lines by either feet or prally.'

Any game of peevers could be transformed into a game of ba' beds by the use of a ball instead of a peever, as the layout of the beds was similar. After the ball was picked up it had to be stotted once and caught in each succeeding bed, and then rolled into the space. This was difficult to manage because, unless it was rolled very gently, the ball was apt to roll too far.

'There were seven in our family', mused Emmie, 'four boys and three girls, and as we played games out-of-doors we were hungry enough not to be fussy about our food, but ate because we were hungry. We would hardly stop our play to go into the house, but used to call out from the back-court: "Mammy, throw us doon a piece an' jeely" – we were fortunate never to have this request refused.'

'Cribbie' is a street game of today which has been devised by boys who live in High Rise flats; having no grass on which to play, they stand facing each other across the street near their home and score points for the ball they throw, according to where it touches – if it hits the kerb (the cribbie) and rolls back, score one point; to catch the rebounding ball on the road, score two points; to catch it on the pavement, score three points, and so on. This is a game they can play near their homes, and there lies much of its value, for boys and girls have always preferred to play in their own street if possible. They are unwilling to go far to reach play facilities provided by the authorities, and mothers, naturally, want the littlins to be within call.

No longer can jeely pieces be thrown out to bairns at play as was the custom in tenements not so very long ago, for, regrettably, 'ye cannae throw pieces oot a twenty storey flat' as the skyscraper wean laments:

I'm a Skyscraper Wean, I live on the nineteenth flair,
But I'm no' gaun oot tae play ony mair.
'Cause since we moved tae Castlemilk I'm wastin' right
    away,
'Cause ma mither's giein' me wan meal less every day.
Chorus:
O, ye cannae fling pieces oot a twenty-storey flat,
Seven hundred hungry weans will testify tae that;
Be it butter, cheese, or jeely, if the breid be plain or pan,
The odds against it reachin' grund are ninety-nine tae wan.

On the first day, ma maw flung oot a piece o' Hovis broon,
It cam' skytin' oot the windae an' went up instead o' doon,
Noo, every twenty-seeven 'oors ma piece comes back in
    sight,
For it went up intae orbit an' becam' a satellite.
Chorus: O, ye cannae, etc.

On the second day, ma maw flung oot a piece wance again,
It went an' hit the pilot o' a fast low-flyin' plane,
He scraped it aff his goggles, shoutin' thro' the intercom,
'The Clyde side Reds have got me with a breid an' jeely
    bomb.'
Chorus: O, ye cannae, etc.

On the third day ma mither thought she'd try anither throw
But the Salvation Army Band wis playin' doon below,
'Onward, Christian Soldiers' wis the piece they should've
    played,
But the oompa man wis playin' on a piece an' marmalade.
Chorus: O, ye cannae, etc.

We've wrote away tae Oxfam tae try an' get some aid,
An' a' the weans in Castlemilk hae joined the Piece Brigade,
We're gaun tae march tae George's Square demandin' civil
   rights,
Like buildin' nae mair hooses ower piece-flingin' height.
Chorus: O, ye cannae, etc.

(Verses from Oral Traditional, collated with that in *The
   Scottish Folk-Singer*, collected and edited by Norman
   Buchan and Peter Hall, Collins, London, 1973. Song
   acknowledged to Adam McNaughton, but no Copyright
   given.)

Ball Games

Stottie ba', hinnie ba', please tell to me
Hoo mony bairns am I to hae?
Yin tae leeve, an' yin tae dee,
An' yin tae sit on the nurse's knee.

Children have always had a wide variety of seasonal games –
special seasons for skipping-ropes, for catapults, bows and
arrows, slings, stilts, and jews' harps which the loons called
their tromps.

The hoop, the kite, and marbles are among the most ancient
of toys, and each generation has had its own version of them
all.

There was a season for stotting balls, at home, in the
playground, or in a quiet village street, children's piping notes
keeping time with the bouncing ball.

Margaret looks back on the individual ball games of her
childhood: 'This is how I played with an old tennis ball, or a
rubber ball about the same size, throwing it against a wall or
door, and catching it, performing in turn each of the
variations, and never allowing the ball to reach the ground:

1 *Plainey* was a simple throw and catch.
2 *Clappy* – throw, clap hands and catch.
3 Throw, turn your back, and catch.
4 Throw and catch with the right hand.
5 Throw and catch with the left hand.
6 *Backy* was when you threw the ball, swinging your arms
behind your back.

7 *Touch ground* – Throw, touch the ground, then catch.
8 *Birl round* – Throw, whirl round, then catch.
9 Throw, then catch in your arms which are folded across your chest.
10 *Roll the Ball* – Throw, roll the hands round each other, then catch.
11 Throw by passing the ball under the right leg, then catch.
12 Do the same with the left leg.
13 *Low Schottische* – Throw, then catch in a cradle made with clasped hands below the waist.
14 *High Schottische* – Throw, and catch in clasped hands held over your head.

Having successfully completed these simple movements, the player usually wished to start all over again, adding a hand-clap to each number. No. 2, Clappy, then required two hand-claps.

'Another variation was to add a Roll the Ball, as well as a Hand Clap, to each number. No. 10 then required the hands to be rolled outwards, then inwards, and then a hand clap before catching the ball. This was possible only when the wall was sufficiently high to ensure that the ball took some time to drop.

'Another game we played by bouncing the ball on the ground, and then against the wall before catching it. This was the routine:

1 Plain throw and catch.
2 Throw under right leg.
3 Throw under left leg.
4 Throw between legs while facing wall.
5 Throw between legs while standing with back to wall.
6 Throw behind back while standing with your side next to the wall.
7 Bounce and throw, using only right hand.
8 Do the same using only left hand.
9 As before, and touch the ground before the catch.
10 Spin round before the catch.

The whole routine could then be repeated with an added hand-clap each time. A third round entailed adding three hand-claps.'

As a child, brought up in Cummertrees, Grace recalls some variations on the individual ball routine. For example:

1 *Clappy Roly* – The hands were clapped and rolled before the catch.
2 *Heady Shoulder* – Touch your head and shoulder before the catch.
3 *Oxter Breesty* – Fold arms across chest, touch breast and catch ball.
4 *Elbow-Knee* – Touch elbow and knee before the catch.
5 *Toey Groundy* – Touch your toe and the ground before the catch.
6 *Birly Jockie* – Whirl right round before catching ball.

If any of these actions are not completed before the catch, or if the ball falls to the ground without being caught, the player must start all over again.

Argyll bairns stotted their ba's through a series of actions which they called 'Plainy', 'Hoppy', 'Skirty' and 'Hairy', the last-named being the movement when the ball was passed through a looped pigtail. Throwing a ball against a wall and catching it was sometimes called 'Capey Clappy', from kepping and clapping. Playing with two balls together was called 'doublers', and with three balls 'throublers'.

An individual ball game with a nonsense-palaver attached was played by Ann at St Monance:

> 'Are you going to golf, Sir?'
> 'No, Sir.'
> 'Why, Sir?'
> 'Because I've got a cold, Sir.'
> 'Where did you get a cold, Sir?'
> 'At the North Pole, Sir!'
> 'What were you doing there, Sir?'
> 'Catching Polar Bears, Sir!'
> 'How many did you catch, Sir?'

It was a game of simple stotting till the 'How many?' question was asked, then it became a succession of 'learies', that is, putting a leg over the ball as it bounced. Another game from Ann was called 'Jinks'. The ball was thrown up against a wall, perhaps the gable-end of a house, and the girl whose name was called had to catch it as it descended. If she missed it she had to fetch it from where it had rolled, and, the rest of the girls having scattered meantime, she had to try to hit one of them with the ball. If she was successful, then that girl had to 'give her farewells', which meant throwing the ball against the wall three times. If it was caught three times that girl was out of the game. If the first girl failed to hit anybody, then *she* had to give her farewells.

In Dalbeattie, in 1917, I came upon a child stotting her ba' and singing:

> One, two, three a-learie,
> Four, five, six a-learie,
> Seven, eight, nine a-learie,
> Ten, a-learie, Postman.

On the first, second, and third a-learies she lifted her right leg neatly over the ball, with an extra lift on the word 'postman'.

With interest I observed her vary the business by repeating the motions with her left leg, then with alternate legs: one, two, three, Right; four, five, six, Left, and so on. I watched her 'stride and jump', that is, jump on the spot with feet together, for ONE, jump astride for TWO, repeating these actions while singing 'a-learie' as before.

Since that far-off day I have heard of many variants; one could be performed only by a girl with pigtails. She brought a pigtail over her left shoulder, grasped it with her right hand, and each time she sang 'a-learie' she stooped forward and as the ball descended it fell through the space created by her bent arm.

'In Dumfries', says Janet, 'instead of "One, two, three a-learie" we sang "One, two, three, Gibraltar" jumping over the ball at the word "Gibraltar", continuing "four, five, six, Gibraltar" without a break.'

Emily recalls that balls in the early days were burstable, with consequent heartache when they were punctured, but then came the unburstable ball, the 'sorbo bouncer' in pastel shades with a powdery bloom on it when it was new, and stotting balls received a new lease of life. 'The games we played by throwing the ball against a wall', says Mary, 'began with reciting the days of the week, Sunday, Monday,

Tuesday, etc., or merely calling out one another's names.
Then came a test of skill with descriptive calls, Keppie,
Clappie, Right and Left Hands, Wee Birlie (the hands were
rolled), Big Birlie (a complete turn round before the catch),
Low Sitation (catching the ball in clasped hands below the
waist), High Sitation (the hands were clasped above the head
with the palms turned outward, ready for the catch). Then the
different joints of the body had to be touched in turn as well as
the head, hand, and foot – and lastly, I think, the ground.'

In Crieff, they sang the same rhyme as in Dalbeattie and
added

> Open the gate and let me through, Sir,
> Open the gate and let me through, Sir,
> Open the gate and let me through, Sir,
> > Early in the morning.

followed by:

> I love coffee,
> I love tea,
> I love the boys,
> And they love me.

In Forfar, Gourdon, and Brechin they sang:

> One, two, three a-learie,
> I saw Maggie Pearie   (Mrs Pearie, or Blearie)
> Sitting on her bum-ba-learie
> Eating chocolate soldiers.

In Ellon they enquired of a stotting ball (as they did in
skipping)

What will my husband be?
  Tinker, tailor, soldier, sailor,
  Rich man, poor man, beggar man, thief?
What shall I be married in?
  Silk, satin, muslin, rags?
What shall we live in?
  Big hoose, little hoose, pig-sty, barn?
Where shall we live?
  Edinburgh, Leith, Portobello, Musselburgh, or Dal-
  keith?

Meg, in Peebles, chanted this rhyme while bouncing her ball against a wall:

> P.K Chewing-gum, tuppence a packet,
> First you suck it, then you crack it,
> Then you stick it on your jacket,
> An' your Ma kicks up a racket,
> P.K Chewing-gum, tuppence a packet!

In Crail they stotted a ball to this rhyme:

> One, two, three, four,
> Mary at the cottage-door,
> Five, six, seven, eight,
> Eating cherries off a plate,
> I've a kistie, I've a creel,
> I've a pokie fu' o' meal,
> Tae gie the bairnies a' their meat,
> Doon fell the summer seat.

This chant came from Fochabers:

> Stot, stot, ba' ba',
> Twenty lassies in a raw,
> No' a lad amang them a',
> Stot, stot, ba' ba'.

but in Arbroath it was:

> Gemm, Gemm, ba' ba'.

In St Andrews they chanted:

> Jenny Myre, blow the fire, puff, puff, puff.

The seventh ball fell on the third puff, and got an extra hard smack, to allow the child to whirl round on her toes and be ready to pat it hard down for the eighth time. A child was once seen to 'blow the fire' twenty-three times in succession!

In Airdrie they stotted the ba' while chanting:

> A house To Let,
> Apply Within.
> A lady put out for selling gin,
> Gin, you know, is a very bad thing;
> So Mary goes out and Jenny comes in.
>   (The ball was then thrown to the girl named.)

57

Sometimes the request was:

Tell me the name of your young man,

his initials being determined by stotting through the alphabet. Then they asked:

What will the engagement ring be?
    Diamonds, rubies, sapphires, pearls?
What conveyance will be used to take them to church?
    Cab, cart, dung-barrow, wheel-barrow?
What will their home be?
    Castle, cottage, house, or midden?

Euphie has not forgotten how boys used to play soccer in their bare feet with a tennis ball in the street in Falkland, and another ball game was to head a tennis ball against a smooth wall without allowing it to fall to the ground. 'I've known a lad head it 300 times without difficulty', she says.

James recalls the game of 'Long Headers', known to Glasgow laddies as 'Lang Heidies'.

'All that was required for this game', he says, 'was a rubber ball, or tennis ball, and a stretch of pavement about twelve feet long. A goal line was marked at each end. A player stood on his goal line, the ball was thrown up and as it descended he headed it towards his opponent at the other end with the object of getting it over the opposing goal-line, the boy at the other end stopping it with hands, feet, or any part of his body and heading it back to the other end. Usually the number of goals was agreed before the start of the game, and the player scoring that number was declared the winner.'

Closes (entrances to tenement buildings) also made good pitches for this game, though balls bouncing off the walls were a nuisance to the ground-floor tenants.

'Short Heidies' was a variation of the above game, a ball and a blank wall being the only requirements. As in Falkland, one player at a time threw the ball in the air and headed it against the wall as many times as he could before missing the ball and letting it fall to the ground. 'Some big scores were recorded', muses James, 'but I usually finished with either a stiff neck or a headache.'

There are several places in Scotland where the traditional

Ba' Game takes place annually, and here, at first hand, is a description from St Ola of the ancient Ba' Game of Orkney which is played on Christmas Day and New Year's Day in Kirkwall.

'There is a Boys' Ba' in the morning', says Marian, 'and a Men's Ba' in the afternoon. There are two teams, the Uppies and the Doonies, depending on which side of the town you were born. I do not know the rules, if any! But both teams meet at the Market Cross in front of St Magnus Cathedral in Kirkwall, where the Ba' is thrown up. Both teams get locked together and push the Ba' either Up or Doon. The Ba' is declared UP if it touches a wall in the upper part of the town. The Doonies win if they manage to get the Ba' in the water at Kirkwall Pier, and they usually follow the Ba' into the water!'

Iain reminds us that 'Shinty is a very old national pastime which at one time enlisted indefinite and unequal numbers, and was practically destitute of rules. Up to forty players on each side played all day, fresh players stepping in now and again from ambush at favourable moments. It has long become an organised game played, not with a wooden ball, as formerly, and knotty sticks, but with recognised shinty sticks, called camans, and a ball of leather. Camans are lighter than hockey sticks. Several are apt to be broken during a game, and the sidesman always has a small sheaf under his arm. The ball is kept in the air as much as possible, and a good two-handed overhead stroke can score from far down the field. It is still played in Tarves, Inveraray, Newtonmore and other places in the Highlands.'

At the turn of the century, Edinburgh schoolgirls in Charlotte Square usually ended a long day in the country engaged in nature study, with a rousing game of rounders, which by them was called 'Dully'. In Crathie, it was called 'Spoonie Hoosie'.

'In Kennoway', says Elizabeth, 'we played rounders like cricket with a bat and ball but no wickets. Whoever was IN had to run from one marked spot to another; if struck by the ball while running, you were OUT.'

Jim remembers that in Dundee, as a change from street football and cricket, the game of 'Beezy' was given a turn. 'The ball being struck by the hand', he explains, 'it was less

Ba' games

likely to cause damage to property. The rules varied according to the wishes of the bigger boys, and whether we had to run between bases, or throw the ball at the runner or the catcher was never satisfactorily established. It was years before I realised that our "Beezy" and its rules were a corruption of baseball.'

I remember playing 'Tether Ball' at Gairnshiel seventy years ago. Edith and I called it 'Bumble Puppy'. It was a game for two players using tennis racquets – old ones, for preference. A tennis ball on a long thin rope was attached to the top of a firm pole about ten feet high, well fixed in the ground. The ball was vigorously hit first by one player and then the other, each trying to wind the cord and the ball round the pole, keeping within an agreed circle and at a certain distance. It was possible at times to send the ball so high and with so much force that it wound round the pole in one stroke, before one's opponent could hit it, and that was the endeavour on both sides.

Orra Ploys an'
Orra Toys

Dae ye min' the shillin' on a string?
I suppose it wis a sneaky thing,
But fan some clutchin' han' got neart,
The coin it up an' disappeart!

'Teach us to delight in simple things', wrote Rudyard Kipling.

'When I see children today being taken everywhere in cars, and provided with transistors, record-players, cameras and much pocket-money, I realise how lucky I was to have lived simply, half-a-century ago, in the lovely countryside of the Borders, even if there was less stress on hygiene – when the cheese was cut in the shop with a wire, the milk and cream taken round the village in churns, and many people used the pumps in the street for water. It was quiet, and the rivers were clean. As my mother used to say, "There's aye somethin'".' So decides Elizabeth.

Let us cast our minds back to some of the 'simple things' that gave pleasure many years ago.

A favourite ploy of city boys, including Jim, was the use of 'sookers'. 'We got a round piece of leather, about two and a half inches across', he says, 'and cut a hole in the middle, through which we passed a length of strong string. We soaked the leather in a dub and made it really wet, then pressed it down hard with a foot. It spread and gripped like a limpet any type of street-grating. With our sookers we lifted gratings clear off the ground and recovered small articles that had fallen through. If anything valuable was spotted under shop-gratings, or 'cundies', as we called them, we used another method. We did not soak our sookers in this case, but applied to their undersides wagon-grease, which we had obtained by stealth from grease-boxes in railway-sidings. In this way we were able to raise the cundies by suction and rescue the objects which had been sighted. Passers-by who had dropped a coin or a brooch would ask for our help; the most common articles that were dropped were hat-pins, and they were the most difficult to recover.

'We also used "dabbers", contrived from a piece of slate or a flat stone attached to a long piece of string, which was a fine ploy, but not so effective as a sooker. We applied wagon-grease to our dabber's underside, or soap if we had no grease, and dropped the dabber through a cellar-grating, hoping to draw up the shining round object which, seen from above, looked like a shilling. If, after long and patient dabbing, we managed to raise it, all too often it proved to be a pearl button, or the round label from the end of a reel of cotton. "Jist a purn-label", we'd groan, and make for home, with cundie-marks all over our faces.'

Out of Nigel's reminiscences came the memory of 'moothies', as mouth-organs were called. 'Lucky lads owned a moothie at some period of their lives, though many a lad who longed to possess one had to do without. Sixpence bought the popular 'Echo' in its tartan box, with the picture on the lid of a boy blowing a horn; longer models cost a bob, and a doublesider cost two bob.'

There were also pea-shooters, pop-guns and water pistols and most boys had peeries, which were pear-shaped tops, usually wound by a string. They had a metal point on which they were set a-spinning and they could be whipped by a leather thong. My father made amusing peeries, using slender-waisted empty pirns cut in half. Having sharpened the cut end to a fine point, he inserted a short stick in the hole, which we held between finger and thumb to send the peerie spinning. The knack lay in causing it to spin steadily on the spot, not to ramble all over the table and tire after a brief spin.

'Shetland children', Elizabeth remembers, 'used to make "snori-banes" from the ankle-bones of a pig. Two loops of string, about eighteen inches long, or as long as a child could

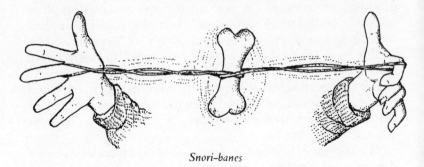

Snori-banes

conveniently hold, were attached to the bane. It was then whirled round, and at once pulled lengthways and slackened. This was repeated, making a snoring sound, the bane whirling like a propeller. A snori could be made with a large-holed button, but it was not so interesting as the bane.'

Dundee laddies, on their way home, sometimes attached a length of string to a school-ruler and spun it round rapidly, producing a variety of buzzing noises as they trotted along. They used to put a coin on the tram-lines (not real money) and see it flattened to double its size by the first tram that came along, and, remembers Jim, 'when the track was on a slope, the stream that ran within the rails after rain provided a wee river on which we raced our matchstick boats.

'We enjoyed wobbling about on an ancient scooter, or rumbling along on one roller-skate. An old bicycle could be hired for fourpence or sixpence an hour . . . a tricycle for a child for about the same figure.

'A small boat and a pair of oars could be hired at the docks at Dundee for sevenpence an hour. The boats were called cobles.

'From between the cassies in hot weather we used to scrape out the tar that bound them together, and made "golf-balls", a messy business!

'We used to dig coags from between the cassies. Coags were metal, chisel-edged pieces inserted in the shoes of the mighty Clydesdales as a means of braking on the steep, granite, cassie-stanes which lined the city streets. The coags were often shed in this gruelling treatment and became lodged between the granite blocks. We made wooden swords, too, and cloth and paper balls for street football; if we had none we just kicked a stone around.'

'In Glasgow it was great to have a barrie or a piler!', James enthuses. 'Why piler? Because every boy in the street wanted to pile into it! It consisted of a wooden box from the grocer, four wheels off an old pram, with a rope attached to the axle of a front wheel to manipulate turning, and there you were! stotting downhill at full speed! Barries were similar to pilers but they had only two wheels and a pair of shafts. We took turns in sitting in the barra for a hurll, and in pushing or pulling another boy between the shafts like a horse.'

Grace remembers the song of a barra that was sung by Glesca' keelies to the tune of 'The British Grenadiers'.

> Ma Uncle Tam tae Glesca' cam
> Alang wi' ma Auntie Jenny,
> He pit his haun intae his pooch
> An' gied me a braw new penny.
> Ah wint tae buy some candy rock
> An' ah fell in wi' O'Hara,
> Ah gied him a sook o' ma candy rock
> For a len o' his braw new barra.
> But noo the bonny wee barra's mines,
> It disnae belang tae O'Hara,
> For the fly wee bloke he stuck tae ma rock,
> Sae ah'm gaunnae stick tae his barra.

Scots bairns have been ca'in' girds almost from the time of the invention of the wheel, but girds and tops are now seldom seen. A really tough ploy in which boys who lived on the outskirts of Glasgow indulged from time to time was to climb to the top of a disused quarry slag-heap, and go tobogganing gaily down on a rusty sheet of bent corrugated iron! In the streets a length of rope tied to a lamp-post became a chair-o-plane for exciting rhythmic swings up and down.

In Edinburgh and elsewhere there was a time when all children played diabolo with sticks about seventeen inches long, and a sort of bobbin or cone about three inches long. The craze was at its height in 1907, but it was not a new invention, but a revival of an old Chinese game. The object of the exercise, requiring skill and practice, was to keep the cone

Yo-Yo and Diábolo

rotating on the string which linked the two sticks, throwing it up in the air and catching it again on the string while it was still spinning. The string was kept slack while the cone was spinning, then quickly made taut to toss the cone aloft. When it fell it was caught on the tightened string, which was immediately slackened and the cone set a-spinning once more. If this was not accomplished at once the cone fell to the ground.

The Yo-Yo, which continues to pass through popularity phases at intervals, first appeared in 1890, under the name of the Bandalore. It consists of two discs united in the centre, having a string wound in the groove formed by the join. 'To work the Yo-Yo', says Annie, 'you must first wind up the string till the groove is filled, then let the toy drop so that the string unwinds. This makes the discs revolve rapidly. Just before they reach the end of the string you must throw your hand gently but firmly upwards so that the Yo-Yo winds up the string in the reverse direction. It can thus be kept flying up and down for any length of time.' Simple as it sounds, we all know how it requires some skill to play it properly, and we admire all the 'Wee Annies' who are so clever in manipulating their individual 'rid Yo-Yo wi' the wee yellow string!'

'Knifie' is an orra ploy which has been known in Scotland for hundreds of years. 'We played it in Nether Dallachy', says Jessie, 'and I cannot recall any mishap occurring through our playing with an open pen-knife, but I dread to think what *might* have happened then, or what might happen today if bairns still indulged in this dare-devil act. We chose a nice flat grassy patch and dug a hole in the middle. We all sat round this hole and with an open pocket-knife did all sorts of intricate movements. In every case the point of the blade had to stand upright in the hole. We tossed the knife off the tips of our fingers, the back of a hand (which we called Backsy), off our fist (which naturally we called Fisty), the elbow, the knee, the forehead, and even off our teeth. We also stuck the knife in the ground, and tried to hit it with the hand and toss it up so that it would land with the blade down in the ground. It was a great ploy!'

Bigton boys made hedgehogs of raw potatoes spiked with matchsticks, and also 'Windy Craas'. To make a Craa also required a medium-sized raw potato which was stuck all over with birds' wing-feathers picked up out-of-doors. They placed the Craa on a flat piece of ground and watched the wind taking it and making it appear to fly away. The more uniform in size the feathers were the better. It was fascinating to watch several Craas as they tumbled along in balls after the manner of tumbleweed.

Grace remembers the fun she had on the stilts her father made for her, and Harriet and Maggie, as children in St Monance, were delighted when they could each obtain two empty syrup-tins from their mothers. They then proceeded to make Tin Feet by piercing a hole in both sides of the tins, threading a long string through the holes, to hold in each hand. 'The string had to be the right length', Maggie emphasises, 'to enable you to stand upright with a foot placed firmly on each upright tin, and on these 'tin feet' you went clumping along holding tightly to the strings.'

'Windy Craas'

'If you were lucky enough to acquire a white clay pipe and a jug of soapy water you could spend a happy afternoon blowing soap bubbles', James remembers. 'We called it "blawin' balloons" and prepared our own mixture with washing-soda an' a wee drap o' glycerine tae mak' the balloons hardier. Then we would lean over the plettie hand-rails and watch our balloons sail awa' ower the slaties an' disappear atween the lummies.'

Dee writes: 'The wash-house door was a natural target for the darts we made by combining a hackle, a cork, and some feathers. In a jute-preparing city like Dundee there were always plenty of hackles lying about, corks were easily come by, and we kept our eyes open for suitable feathers.

'To make a parachute you took your hankie and tied a large washer to the four corners with thin thread. When you tossed the hankie in the air from the pletties, it opened out like a real parachute, and was rescued on landing by arrangement with a pal, who brought it back, shouting as he came up the stairs, "Gie's a shottie!" Then it was his turn.

'We often found a tattie-gun in a Penny Lucky Bag. It was a thin metal tube about four inches long. With it went a pusher – a metal pin which fitted into the tube. Ammunition for the tattie-gun was obtained by pushing the tube a little way into a raw potato, and pressing the pellet out with the pusher. A battle between tattie-guns and pea-shooters was rare fun.'

'A ploy for which a look-out had to be kept for the patrolling policeman was known to us as Boom-a-Rone', says George. 'Some tissue-paper would be shoved loosely up a drain-pipe at the side of a house, and set alight. In a second or two a loud booming noise awoke the echoes both outside and inside the house, and the drain-pipe would shudder. It was tremendous fun, but woe betide us if the Law caught us at it. The look-out was supposed to yell "A.B.C.", which stood for "Auchterarder, Bobbie's coming!", but at times he was so engrossed in the ploy he failed to notice the approach of the Bobbie.'

Malcolm says: 'We made little bombs from small domed pieces of metal. We put a percussion cap between the metal domes and dropped the bomb on to the pavement behind some unsuspecting old lady. We played other tricks, e.g., I've seen fun with a purse tied to a long piece of strong thread and left lying on the ground. We would hide where we could watch without being seen, and when some passer-by stooped to lift it we whisked the purse away.'

'Purns were empty reels obtained at the spinning-mill', Dee remembers. 'We boys notched the ends and attached a piece of string, then dirled them on people's windows and ran. A door opened – there was no one there.'

Mischievous boys in Tarves played a similar trick by tying a button on a long thread to a cottage window. They made the button tap at the window while they hid behind a bush. It was sometimes possible to do the same with something tied to a door-handle. Sandy describes yet another method: 'With a screw about an inch long passed through a rubber washer from the neck of a bottle, and a piece of string, knotted at intervals, tied to the pointed end of the screw we lads prepared to trick the householder. The washer was moistened and the contraption stuck to a window. By running the hand along the knots in the string, a fast rickety-tickety noise could be played against the window from a safe distance. The alarmed householder could not at first detect where the noise was coming from. Some of the more adventurous boys would

Little bombs

select two doors facing each other in a tenement close, and with a length of stout rope tie the two door-knobs together, then drum loudly on both doors. In theory, the residents would dash to their respective doors and pull hard (in opposite directions). What actually happened I'll never know for I ran so fast and so far on my little fat legs, and stayed away so long, that it was all over long before my cautious return.'

'In the dark evenings', Bill recalls, 'we sometimes contrived a sort of heater by punching holes in the lid and bottom of a cocoa-tin, then stuffing it with rags and paper, replacing the lid, and setting the rags alight before doing so. We wrapped a cloth round the tin to protect our hands from the heat; we ran making "puff–puff" noises, pretending to be either a railway-engine or a donkey-engine, while holding the home-made stove aloft, and a trail of smoke and sparks issued from the smouldering contents. It was even better if we could get a drop of oil or grease on the rags, and soon the street was filled with smoke from a dozen or so smelly little cans.'

'If we found a discarded cylindrical tin of calcium carbide (used for gas lamps)', James says, 'we added a little water to what was left in the tin, set a lighted match to the carbide, and BANG!'

'I was a great one for making cannons and pistols out of gas piping', says Malcolm. 'We used black powder. They must have been highly dangerous and quite illegal. Some boys, unknown to their parents, melted the Coronation medals they had been given by holding them over the kitchen fire in an iron spoon. They made fine sinkers for their fishing-lines.'

70

Mark inherited a box of plain wooden building-blocks from his grandfather. They had been beautifully made by hand, stained and polished by a carpenter who loved children. He also had picture-blocks, an elementary introduction to the jig-saws of later years. He possessed one of those treasured clasp-knives with adequate equipment for taking stones out of horses' hooves, not to mention card games like 'Animal Grab' which date from the 1890s, and a collection of cigarette cards which, in Glasgow, were known as 'Fag Picters' or 'Cig Photies'. Of the same period were puzzles in small glazed boxes with a maddening silver ball, bent wires, and solid fragments of metal, all refusing to co-operate.

Robert and his friends often bought packets containing two or three pictures of contemporary footballers from stationers for about a penny or a ha'penny a packet. The pictures were printed on heart-shaped paper about the size of a beer-bottle label. The boys' ambition was to acquire as many pictures as possible, but not by buying them as they could not afford to do that; so, apart from the usual method of swopping them, they devised the following game: the first player placed one of his pictures flat on the playground-wall (about two or three feet from the ground) and let it fall gently to the ground. The next player placed one of his pictures on the wall but not necessarily at the same place – he could move it to the right or left according to where he felt it had the best chance of falling on to the first player's picture. He then released his picture and if he was lucky, or skilful enough, it would fall on the first picture which he would pick up and retain. This did not happen often, but, as the game progressed, and several players had dropped their pictures, there were greater chances of a picture landing on one on the ground. When this happened the player not only secured a picture but was allowed another 'shot'. A fair number of pictures changed hands in the course of a game, and at one time it was very popular.

'We used to buy a sheet of Dabbities (transfers) for a ha'penny a sheet to put in a jotter', Emma remembers, 'quite often we stuck them on the backs of our hands where these coloured pictures would remain even after washing. "Scraps" were pictures made of stout paper, beautifully coloured. It was possible to buy for a ha'penny a sheet of Flower Scraps,

71

Fairies, or Angels, or perhaps Children Dressed in Party Frocks. We got a lot of enjoyment while exchanging scraps, all aiming at having the best collection in the school.'

When my sister and I felt like dancing, as we often did of a winter evening, my mother would diddle for us. She must have devised her own variation of one of the traditional tunes which are diddled in the Western Isles, and have been revived for dancing at some Highland Gatherings. It is literally 'mouth music' and we loved to twirl round in imitation of Highland dancers till we collapsed, breathless and laughing, in our chairs.

'A game we played, which was surely born of a need for economy', Mary relates, 'began with cutting out pictures and figures from Mail Order catalogues, or any other suitable source. These were inserted between the pages of a large book. The covers were held tightly together, then we offered our friends a pin to insert somewhere between the leaves. The book was then opened at that place. If a picture cut-out was revealed, the pin-holder was allowed to keep it; if not, she had to surrender the pin to the holder of the book, who wore it on her dress or coat. The aim was to display a large frontage of pins! We always had access to plenty of books, my father being the village schoolmaster, and there was always a directory or something of the sort.'

'Coloured scraps, bought for about a penny a dozen, we scattered between the pages of a thick book, or discarded telephone directory', Ena remembers, 'and with these we played Three and a Blinkie, which meant that we allowed our friends to have three goes at opening the book at a page where lay a scrap – if lucky, they could keep the scrap. An extra go was allowed with eyes shut; that is, a "blinkie". Girls played with scraps; boys used cigarette cards.'

In Sanquhar they played the game with cut-out pictures from magazines. They offered a book and said 'Dab with a pin'. If the pin went in where a picture was, they got it; if not, they had to hand over the pin. The rhyme the Sanquhar bairns used was:

> Dab a preen in my lottery book,
> Dab ane, dab twa,
> Dab a' yer preens awa'.

Gourdon bairns were taught the art of paper-folding and paper-cutting at school, cutting coloured squares into elaborate patterns, framing photographs, and making paper boats.

'At the end of World War I we had no lovely dolls', says Bessie, 'so we took wooden clothes pegs with round tops and made peg dollies. We used to beg cuttings of dress material from the village dressmaker to make clothes for our dollies. Mother's old curtains came in handy for us dressing up in our finery. Bairns have always enjoyed dressing up. When we were dressed in our best we wore long white drawers, and it was fashionable to let the crochet trimming show below the hem of the dress. We wore two petticoats, a striped one and a white starched one trimmed with crochet lace; and a pinny to keep our frock clean. I was in the same class at school as Jimmy Shand. He was always a quiet shy boy.'

'I remember an incident at school in Fife when I was five or six', says Betty. 'It must have been the occasion of a Coronation or some other national celebration. We were each given a new school-bag, and were allowed to choose a doll. When I took my doll home it was put on a shelf as an ornament and I was not allowed to play with it; but when we had friends to stay, a little girl wanted "a wee play" with the doll and broke it. It was a china doll, dressed in white, very lovely, but only a memory now.'

'I remember, before the First World War', says Elizabeth, 'the shops in Shetland sold, very cheaply, little Japanese dolls, very dainty though made of wood, painted and dressed in brightly-coloured paper; and little girls also had dolls made of straw, neatly made, and boys had roughly-carved little boats.'

Ina recalls her childhood in Aberdeen and the clootie doll which her grannie made for her which was about three feet high, nearly as big as herself. Her name was Sally, and she had black velvet boots, and was beloved by all the children in the neighbourhood. When a child was sick, the mother would come to beg the loan of Sally for an hour or two to comfort her. On these occasions Ina's mother would give Sally a thorough wash on her return, in case of any kind of infection from the sick child, and Sally was re-dressed once again, Grannie gladly providing her with a complete outfit of fresh

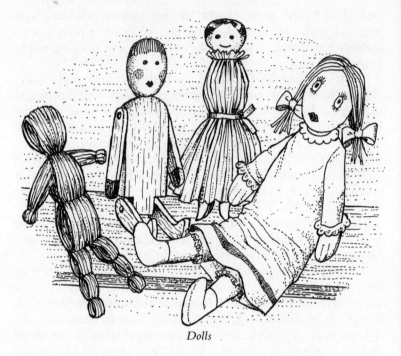

Dolls

clothing from time to time. Sally was Ina's treasure for many years and the joy of all her little friends, and when the time came for the inevitable parting. Sally in her velvet boots became the darling adopted child of the bairns in a Children's Home.

'The only home-made dolls I remember in Bressay', says Stella, 'were rag dolls known as "dukkies" (Norwegian for doll is *dukke*). These could be simple or elaborate, according to the ideas of their creator.'

We had cardboard cut-out dolls with numerous gaily-coloured changes of costume, with tags which fitted on the front; we also had various rubber animals, unpainted, which had a small metal button inserted on the underside. This provided a squeak when the toy was squeezed. Penny toys made from scraps of material were trifles sold by street hawkers. Off and on, throughout the year, we collected empty cotton-reels, the stout ones on which linen thread used to be wound. These we painted bright red with bands of green just before Christmas, and with a sprig of greenery stuck in the little 'barrel' we had miniature Christmas Trees for table decoration. A series of small, slender-waisted cotton-reels glued together in columns of three and enamelled in gay colours made attractive holders for Christmas candles. Cotton-reels, scrubbed and strung on a piece of strong string, often kept the baby in his pram amused for quite a long time.

'Father made us lovely toys,' says Jessie, 'I remember "Acky Davies" made from two upright pieces of wood with string stretched between them. A mannie, fashioned from separate pieces, the arms and legs jointed, was threaded on to the cross string. When the two upright sides were pressed together Little Acky Davy danced and did acrobatics.

'Another toy I remember we called Petery Dicks. To make it, Father took a piece of wood about an inch and a half long and an inch deep with one side cut out, and a length of string with a short wooden peg held firmly by twisting the string. We held this toy between the thumb and first finger of the right hand, and the taut pin strummed with the fingers of the left hand made a rhythmic sound.'

A song about a toy-shop was a favourite solo at 'Sorees' in the early 1900s. It was called 'The Tin Gee-Gee', and was written and composed by Fred Capes (*c.* 1890):

> I was strolling one day down the Lowther Arcade,
> That place for children's toys,
> Where you may buy a dolly or a spade
> For your good little girls and boys.
> And as I passed a certain stall,
> Said a little wee voice to me,
> 'O, I am a Colonel in a little cocked hat
> And I ride on a tin gee-gee.
> O, I am a Colonel in a little cocked hat
> And I ride on a tin gee-gee.'
>
> Then I looked, and a little tin soldier I saw
> In his little cocked hat so fine,
> He'd a little tin sword that shone in the light
> As he led a glittering line
> Of tin hussars whose sabres flashed
> In a manner a la militaire-ee,

Whilst that little tin soldier he rode at their head
So proud on his tin gee-gee.
Whilst that little tin soldier he rode at their head
So proud on his tin gee-gee.

Then that little tin soldier he sobbed and he sighed,
So I patted his little tin head,
'What vexes your little tin soul?' said I,
And this is what he said.
'I've been on this stall a very long time
And I'm marked one-and-nine, you see,
While just on the shelf above my head
There's a fellow marked two-and-three.
While just on the shelf above my head
There's a fellow marked two-and-three.

Now he hasn't got a sword and he hasn't got a horse
And I'm quite as good as he,
Then why mark me at one-and-nine
And him at two-and-three?
There's a pretty little dolly-girl over there,
And I'm madly in love with she,
But now that I'm only marked one-and-nine
She turns up her nose at me.
She turns up her nose at one-and-nine
And flirts with two-and-three.

And O, she's dressed in a beautiful dress,
A dress I do admire,
She has pearly blue eyes that open and shut
When worked inside by a wire.
And, once on a time, when the folks had gone,
She used to ogle me,
But now that I'm only marked one-and-nine
She turns up her nose at me,
She turns up her little wax nose at me
And carries on with two-and-three.'

'Cheer up, my little tin man', said I,
'I'll see what I can do,
You're a fine little fellow, and it is a shame
That she should so treat you!'

So I took down the label from the upper shelf
And I labelled him two-and-three,
And I marked the other one one-and-nine,
Which was very very wrong of me;
But I felt sorry for that little tin soul
As he rode on his tin gee-gee,
I felt so sorry for that little tin soul
As he rode on his tin gee-gee.

Now that little tin soldier
He puffed with pride
At being marked two-and-three,
And that saucy little dolly-girl smiled once more,
For he'd risen in life, you see!
And it's so in this world – for I'm in love
With a maiden of high degree,
But I'm only marked at one-and-nine,
And the other chap's two-and-three.
And a girl never looks at one-and-nine
With a possible two-and-three,
A girl never looks at one-and-nine
With a possible two-and-three!

Marjory says 'When I was a little girl I recall that I used to sit with my grand-mother piercing Morello Cherries with a darning needle. She immersed them in brandy and made a liqueur which was a beautiful colour when it was decanted. It was offered to guests the following year at Christmas and the New Year, and at all family festivals.'

Emma's memories are chiefly of the years between 1897 and 1918. 'At the tram-car terminus beside Glasgow University', she says, 'the tram stopped for about ten minutes and girls and boys were allowed on board. We gathered the discarded tram tickets of various colours and made them into neat bundles, each of us trying to see who could collect the most. There were no collecting-boxes for used tickets prior to 1914, tickets were simply thrown on the floor. On Sundays, after church, especially in Summertime, we would board the tram-car, dressed in our best clothes, and have a run down to Charing Cross, for which we paid a ha'penny. Then we walked home very sedately. It was quite an adventure for ten-year-olds. On

Midden raking

78

Sunday afternoon we would be given a poke of stale bread. We walked to Kelvingrove Park and were very happy throwing bread to the clamouring, cackling ducks. Another thing that gave us great pleasure was to take a little sister or brother to school in the afternoon of any week-day if our Mother had shopping to do in Town. We were allowed to do this by the teacher in those days. The littlin often caused a lot of amusement among the pupils, and the afternoon passed very quickly! I also remember that, in those early days in Glasgow, ashes from household fires and all sorts of rubbish were emptied into middens in the back-courts. Poorly-clad men and women used to go around with sacks on their backs, and cleeks, or muck-rakes, in their hands, raking through the middens to see if they could find anything worth saving and selling, poor souls!

'From this custom arose a saying among school-children; if you had fallen out with your best friend and felt spiteful towards her you might shout after her "Rake the Midden" which was the most dreadful insult, and go off, nonchalantly humming a popular song, such as that wartime jingle:

> Ye cannae shove yer grannie aff a bus,
> Ye cannae shove yer grannie aff a bus,
> Ye cannae shove yer grannie
> For she's yer mammy's mammy,
> Ye cannae shove yer grannie aff a bus.

> Ye can shove yer ither grannie aff a bus,
> Ye can shove yer ither grannie aff a bus,
> Ye can shove yer ither grannie
> For she's yer faither's mammy,
> Ye can shove yer ither grannie aff a bus.

Leah remembers in her pre-school days how a Rag and Bone man called regularly with his donkey-cart, with a Dalmatian dog following. These were known as Gentlemen's dogs, following his lordship's carriage. This one was very kindly treated by his master, an old soldier with an iron hook for a hand, of which I was much afraid. He took a noontide rest and when he returned from the 'local', it was my delight to see him take Daisy the Donkey's nose-bag off and tell Prince

the Dog to kiss Daisy. I gave Daisy many lumps of sugar and
there was always a bone for Prince. I well remember the day in
1901 when Queen Victoria died . . . no telephone, no radio
then. My eldest sister received telegrams on an A.B.C.
instrument from Head Office in Stockport. A Public Notice
was pinned up for all to see. I remember that at the time I was
playing a noisy game of 'Liberals and Tories' with my brother.
We were told to Hush immediately – 'Queen Victoria is dead!'

Emmie also remembers figures from the past who are no
longer with us. "There was the Chapper, the man who ran
round the houses in the early morning, calling on his clients
who paid him a small fee to waken early by chapping on
their doors, or windows, to get them up in time to make their
way to the factory, and I have never forgotten the boy who
used to run behind horse-drawn vehicles with a bucket and
shovel, collecting manure for his mother's garden. Leerie the
Lamplighter is another unforgettable figure – we knew a
rhyme about him:

> Leerie, leerie, licht the lamps!
> Lang legs an' crooked shanks!
> Tak a stick an' brak his back
> An' send him tae Kirkcaldy!

There was the lad in the ballad who wanted to emigrate, but
his mother would not hear of it. To all his pleas she replied:

> No, No, No, Geordie Munro,
> No, No, No, ma wee laddie!
> Ye maunna go tae Idaho
> Ye'd better bide here in Kirkcaddy!

But the best-known of all the verses that involve Kirkcaldy
is 'The Boy in the Train'.

Mabel C. Smith, a Dumfries lady who was born in 1869,
wrote the ever-popular 'The Boy in the Train', which was
recently given an honoured place in the Merchiston College
Magazine. Incidentally, the 'queer-like smell' of linoleum in
the making, which used to dominate Kirkcaldy railway
station, is no longer noticeable. Now, hearken to the words of
the boy in the train on his way with his parents to visit his

gran'ma, and as restless and inquiring as a normal small boy
can be:

Whit wey does the engine say Toot–toot?
Is it feart to gang in the tunnel?
Whit wey is the furnace no pit oot
When the rain gangs doon the funnel?
What'll I hae for my tea the nicht?
A herrin', or maybe a haddie?
Has Gran'ma gotten electric licht?
Is the next stop Kirkcaddy?

There's a hoodie-craw on yon turnip-raw!
An' sea-gulls! sax or seeven.
I'll no fa' oot o' the windae, Maw,
It's sneckit, as sure's I'm leevin'.
We're in the tunnel! We're a' in the dark!
But dinna be frichtit, Daddy,
We'll sune be comin' to Beveridge Park,
An' the next stop's Kirkcaddy!

Is yon the mune I see in the sky?
It's awfu' wee an' curly,
See! there's a coo an' a cauf ootbye,
An' a lassie pu'in' a hurly!
He's chackit the tickets an' gi'en them back,
Sae gie me my ain yin, Daddy,
Lift doon the bag frae the luggage-rack,
For the next stop's Kirkcaddy!

There's a gey wheen boats at the harbour-mou',
And eh, dae ye see the cruisers?
The cinnamon-drop I was sookin' the noo
Has tummelt an'·stuck tae ma troosers . . .
I'll sune be ringin' ma Gran'ma's bell,
She'll cry, 'Come ben, my laddie!'
For I ken masel' by the queer-like smell
That the next stop's Kirkcaddy!

Counting-out Rhymes

Eetum Peetum penny pump
A' the leddies in a lump
Sax or seeven in a clew
An' a' made wi' gundy glue.

Before the start of play, of course, there had to be some counting-out. Counting-out rhymes, as a method of choosing players or sides, form one of the most interesting topics in the study of children's games. They are as old as history, having come down, like the great mass of the games of childhood, from the important practices of their elders. The same rhymes are used over a wide area; bairns have delighted in these jingles for far longer than even the oldest grandparent can recall. Some apparently nonsensical versifications are believed to be of classical origin, but then bairns have always been perfectly happy to recite and remember (better than school-lessons) a string of words that appear to make no sense at all. There are thousands of gibberish chants, such as this from Kirkcaldy:

Ra, ra, chuckeree, chuckeree,
Ony pony, ningy, ningy, na,
Addy, caddy, westoe,
Anty poo,
Chutipan, chutipan,
China chu.

And this from Glasgow:

> Ra, ra, twekers,
> Ronee, ponee,
> In-a, kin-a, na,
> In-a, kin-a, weskin-a,
> Anti-poo, Eetie-poo,
> Cheeti-pan,
> Chinie-choo.

The ritual performed as a prelude to almost any game could be as much fun as the game itself; for example, when players were lined up against a wall with fists outheld to be slapped down in turn by the counter-out who chanted at speed:

> One potato, two potato, three potato, four,
> Five potato, six potato, seven potato, more,

the littlins were often so entranced by the performance they forgot what game they were about to play. (As mentioned earlier (p. 26) school-girls used this rhyme when making a column with closed fists.)

In every counting-out rhyme, the child on whom the last word fell was OUT; at each repetition of the words another child fell out; the last one had to be IT, HIT, HET, HUT, or TALKIE, depending on the local designation, the others having been chappit or tittit out.

One player did the counting-out, repeating the favoured jingle of the district, touching, or pointing at, one player for every accented word.

In our Glen we lined up against the school wall, and the counter-out pointed briefly at each bairn while gabbling a rhyme till all but one were eliminated, and that one had to be HIT. Not for us the common 'Eeny, meeny, miney, mo', not even the familiar 'Eetle, Ottle, Black Bottle'. We liked our own version of the rhyme that Pet Marjorie taught Sir Walter Scott, which was

> Wonery, twoery, tickery, seven,
> Alaby, crackaby, ten and eleven,
> Ping, pang, Musky dan,
> Tweedilum, toodle-um, twenty-wan.

Marjorie Fleming, Scott's little friend, died four days after her eighth birthday. She has been called 'the youngest Immortal in the World of Literature' and wrote amazing little poems for one of such tender years. Her original head-stone is let into the back of the modern pedestal, the white marble cross in Abbotshall Churchyard, Kirkcaldy.

A Deeside variation of 'Eeny, meeny, miney, mo' was:

> Eeny, meeny, clean peeny,
> If you want a piece an' jeely,
> You-walk-out!

There are many variations on the theme of 'Eetle, Ottle, Black Bottle'. Edinburgh bairns added:

> Tea and sugar is my delight,
> And O-U-T spells OUT.

Kirkcaldy jeered:

> If you had been where I had been,
> You would no' have been out.

And Troon chanted this addition:

> Like a silver threepenny piece
> Shining on the mantelpiece.

When a verse was not long enough to go round the entire group of children, the counter-out was entitled to extend it by adding 'One, two, three, Out goes he' (or she), by spelling O-U-T spells Out, or by using any other method that occurred to him, though the other bairns liked to know at the outset what method he was going to use. In Angus, for example, they frequently added:

> Toosh out, toosh in,
> Toosh upon a rolling-pin,
> Black fish, white trout,
> Eerie, Orrie, You are to be put out,
> Out of this G-A-M-E, game, game,
>   game!

The words used long ago by shepherds in counting sheep have been recalled. Women used them too, in counting their knitting stitches, so, naturally, bairns followed their example, imitating the words to the best of their ability.

The best-known method of counting sheep was

Yan, tan, tethera, methera, pimp.
Sethera, lethera, levers, dovers, dick.
Yanadick, tanadick, tetheradick, metheradick, bumfit.
Yanabumfit, tanabumfit, tetherabumfit, metherabumfit,
    giggot.

Another version was:

Yan, tan, tethera, pethera, pimp,
Sethera, lethera, hovera, covera, dick,
Yanadick, tanadick, etc.

Now see what the bairns made of it!
In Tranent they did their best with this:

Eenery, eatery, hethery, methery,
Bamfry, eatery, cheetery, overy, dovery,
Ding dong bell, on my nell,
An pan toosh,
Out goes the bonnie lass,
Out goes she.

In most places, the words 'One, two, three, you are OUT', or similar wording, were added to every rhyme, and need not be repeated here.

From Gullane came this:

Eenty, teenty, tethera, methera,
Bam-full-ery, hover, dover,
Ell, dell, dominell,
Ram tam, toosy Jock.

Robert, aged 98, writing from his home in Montreal, assures me that counting-out in Aberdeen in the early 1900s went something like this:

Up a lether,
Doon a brae,
A penny loaf'll ser' a' day.

Can ye crack a biscuit?
Can ye smoke a pipe?
Can ye kiss a bonny lass
At twelve o'clock at night?
Auld rags mak' paper – you are OUT!

This came from Ena whose grandmother, born in 1860, handed it down:

Zeenty, teenty, jiggery, fell,
Ell, dell, dominell,
Urky, purky, tawry rope,
An, tan, toosy joke.

In the West of Scotland they used this rhyme:

Zeenty, meenty, Fickery, Fick,
Deal, dell, dominick,
Zanty, panty, on a rock,
Ran, tan, toosh Jock.

In Arbroath it was:

Ingerty, fingerty, fickerty, fay,
Ell, dell, dominay
Inky, pinky, starry rock,
Jock oot, Jock in,
Jock through a heckle pin.

A Dundee version went:

Eenty, feenty, figurey, fegg,
Ell, dell, dominegg.
Irky, birky, starry rock,
An, tan, toose, Jock.
Jock oot, Jock in,
Jock through the pocket-pin.
Tak' a mell an' knock them ower,
One, two, three fower.

In Torphins they added:

Tak' a rusty nail an' push him oot,
Oot for supper, bread an' butter.

The Montrose version was a little different:

> Eenerty, feenerty, figgerty, fegg,
> Ell, dell, dominegg,
> Irky, birky, stoorie rock,
> An, tan, choose, chock,
> Black pudding, white trout,
> Eerie, orrie, you are OUT.

James, writing from Pittsburg, Pennsylvania, recalls a counting-out rhyme from his school-days (1912-25) at the little school at Haiton, near Kelso:

> One-ery, two-ery, tickery teeven,
> Alamy, crackaby, ten an' eleeven,
> Spin, span, masky dan,
> Teedle-um, toodle-um, twenty-wan,
> Black pudding, white trout, Eerie, orrie, you are OUT!

In Kinross they said:

> Eenty, teenty, nithery, bithery,
> Bamfie, eevie, shutri, kutri,
> Ding, dong, simonell,
> Tom, tom, toosh pipes.

This one came from Edinburgh:

> Inty, tinty, tethery, methery,
> Bank for over, dover, ding,
> Aut, taut, toosh,
> Up the Causey, doon the Cross,
> There stands a bonnie white horse,
> It can gallop, it can trot,
> It can carry the mustard-pot.

So did this:

> Eenty, teenty, Beverley Bell,
> Ell, dell, dominell,
> Irky, pirky, tammy now,
> Am, tam, toosy Joe.

Elsa writes, 'When I was a teenager in the late '40s, my family was very friendly with a retired sea-captain called

Captain Crocker, who lived at Strone on the Holy Loch. He originally came from Irvine or Girvan, and ran away to sea at the age of thirteen to sail before the mast. He was born in 1870. He taught me this counting-out rhyme:

> A-zeenty, teenty, heathery, methery, bethery,
> Bumpty, sugary, hovey, dovey,
> Saw the Laird of Heaslem Peaslem
> Jumpin' ower Methuselah's dyke,
> Playin' on his wee
> Pee-pi-po-puddock-pipe.

From Kirkcudbright came yet another:

> Eenty, teenty, tenery, menery,
> Bamfo, leetery, hover, dover,
> Saw the King o' Hazel Pazel,
> Jumpin' ower Jerusalem dykes,
> Playin' on his wee bagpipes.

Graham says 'My grandfather told my father, who was born in 1866, that this was the old counting-out rhyme in Dundee in his school-days, and, for some reason, he was of the opinion that it was French in derivation:

> Ennerty, Fennerty, Fickerty, Fegg
> Ell, dell, dominegg,
> Din, dan, must be done,
> Hollerby, crackerby, twenty-one.

In Shetland and in the streets and open spaces of Aberdeen they chanted:

> Eenery, twa-ery, tuckery teeven,
> Hal-a-ba, crackery, ten an' eleeven,
> Peen, pan, musky dan,
> Feedalam, faddalum, twenty-wan.

But Leith preferred:

> Pin, Pan, Dusty Man,
> Tiddle-um, toddle-um, twenty-one.

or

> Pip, pop, must be done,
> Nickabo, nickabo, twenty-one.

Methlick's chant made a change:

> One-ery, two-ery, tickery, ten,
> Bobs of vinegar, gentle-men,
> A bird in the air, a fish in the sea,
> A bonnie wee lassie comes singin' tae thee.

Counting-out rhymes in Airdrie were:

As I went up the ecky pecky road
I met some ecky pecky people
What colour were they dressed in! Red?
R-E-D spells red and O-U-T spells OUT, and out you must go!

also:

> As I went up the ecky pecky road
> I met a scabby donkey,
> You one it, you two it, you three it,
> You four it, you five it, you six it, you seven it, you ATE it!

For a real time-saver there was nothing to beat:

> Eetle, Ottle, Black Bottle,
> Eetle, Ottle, Oot!

except, perhaps, Glasgow's

> Oot, Scoot, you're Oot.

Or Aberdeen's gabble of

> Horsie, cairtie, rummle oot!

In Gourdon they counted out like this:

> Eesie, osie, mannie's nosie, eesie, osie, oot!
> I pick you for a penny dish-clout!

And in the West of Scotland:

> Eese, Ose, Man's Nose,
> Cauld parritch, pease brose.

(The 'man' or 'mannie' was the name sometimes given to the last one out, who had to be HIT.)

Forfar bairns were original in their counting-out:

> Eener, awner, Kirsty Gaumer
> Doon in Carnoustie, merchant daller,
> Leddy Celestie, Sandy Testie,
> Bonny poppy-show, You are OUT!

In Crieff they chanted:

> Eatum, peatum, potum, pye,
> Babylonie, stickum, sty,
> Dog's tail, hog's snout,
> I'm IN, you're OUT!

But in the remote Isle of Foula it was:

> Eetum, peetum, penny pie,
> Jirkin, jury, jenny, ji,
> White fish, black troot,
> Gibbie ga, an' DU's OOT!

and

> Eetum, peetum, penny pump,
> All da leddies in a lump,
> Wan, two, three,
> Out goes she!

Annan bairns, to be different, counted this way:

> Ibbity, bibbity, nibbity, nap,
> Ibbity, bibbity, kinella, knack,
> Kinella up, kinella down,
> Ibbity, bibbity, nibbity, sap.

Aberdeen struck a new note with

> I saw a doo flee ower the lum
> Wi' siller wings an' gouden bum,
> She lookit east, she lookit west,
> She lookit far tae licht the best.

Angus bairns said

> Eerie, orrie, ower the dam,
> Fill yer poke an' let's gang.

'This game, "Pickin' da Mill"', says Elizabeth, 'was exclusive to the Isle of Foula where I taught at one time. It is my favourite counting-out rhyme from Shetland, and surely the oldest in Britain. It refers to the mill-stone, so necessary in olden times to grind the corn. Every now and then they were examined and pickit, that is, roughened. In the game the children stood in a row and recited this rhyme:

> Fower an' twenty millstanes stude alang da wa',
> Wisna he a gude picker 'at cud pick dam a',
> Pick wan, pick twa.

('Picking' rapidly along the line, till the picker touched one, who thereupon became the picker.) I think the idea was to see how many he could "pick" in one breath!'

Instead of saying

> Soldier, Sailor, Tinker, Tailor,
> Rich man, Poor Man, Beggar-man, Thief,

a jingle which is known everywhere, Aberdeen bairns used to count their Father's waistcoat buttons to this jingle:

> Lord and Laird,
> Piper, Drummer,
> Rich man, Thief
> Of Angus Beef!

a reference to the famous breed of Aberdeen-Angus cattle. And in Angus, the same rhyme was used to count plumstones round a plate:

> A Laird, a Lord,
> A Rich man, a Thief,
> A Piper, a Drummer,
> A Stealer of Beef.

Games in the
Playground

Have you any bread and wine?
We are the Rovers.
Have you any bread and wine,
For we're the gallant sojers?

When the counting-out had been done and it had, therefore,
been decided who should be Hit or It (or Het), any one of a
score of hard-fought games could follow. Chasing games are
founded on the ancient custom of The Hunt, and always
involve two teams to play the hunters and the hunted, those
who chase and those who are chased, and a den or dell which is
a place of safety, the end of the game being the bringing home
of the captives like the end of the chase.

'"Old Bull" was mainly a girls' game', says Rosamond, 'it
required plenty of space. The girl who was Het had to chase
the others, and when she caught one they joined hands and
together chased the rest. As each girl was caught she joined the
chasers, till, eventually, there was a long line tearing round
trying to bring the last girl in. The game was seldom played by
boys.'

Dorothea remembers, 'During the 80's and 90's a Dame's
School was kept by two sisters, the Misses Bowman, in Old
Aberdeen. Generations of children, mainly from professional
families, received their early education, and a good one, too, at
"Miss Bo'am's", as it was called by the youngest pupils. A
very old game, described in the *Scottish National Dictionary*,
was played at that school, called "Hunt the Staigie" or "Hunty
Unity Staigie". One child was chosen to be the Staigie, the

others scattered throughout the large garden. The staigie locked his fingers together and chanted

> Hunt the Staigie,
> Huntie, Unity, Staigie,
> Alleman, alleman, aigie,

and went off to find the other children, with the fingers of both hands still interlocked. Until he caught somebody he could not unlock his fingers, but when he did, they joined hands and together hunted the others. This went on till all were caught.' Several pupils of 'Miss Bo'am's' remember The Staigie clearly.

'The staigie was, of course, a horse . . . frequently a stallion', David explains, 'Alleman (or Elliman) aigie' is a childish corruption of a phrase, "the last element is naigie". A naigie was a little nag, and the whole game appears to have been a reference to some kind of Hunt or Chase on horse-back.'

All forms of 'Tig' were popular but perhaps 'Lame Tig' caused the most amusement, for the tigged girls had to hold with one hand the part of their body that had been tigged, and in some comical positions had to continue to run. Robert, an Aberdonian, recalls the game of 'Cock-a-Roostie' in which the boy who was Het was handicapped by having to attempt to tig someone with his hands clasped. (Tig was 'tackie' in Crathie.) When he managed to tig a boy they joined hands and chased another victim, who, when caught, had to join hands with them. Part of the fun was to get behind the chasers and try to break their line, whereupon they were buffed back to their den by the other players using their 'bunnets', and had to start all over again. Robert says it was *great fun* especially when the two lines were about equal, and a real Bunnet Battle ensued.

Iain conjures up the accepted playground game at Glasgow Academy at the time of the First World War. It was called 'Bar the Door'. All it required was ample running space in a quiet road or playground. The leader called 'Last across for Bar the Door', and the last boy to reach the indicated wall had to be Het. He then stood in the middle of the playground and called by name any boy he chose, and that boy had to try to cross to the opposite wall without being caught. Dodging and handing off, as in Rugby, were permissible, but not fighting. If he was caught he stayed with the first boy and both called out the others by name until one boy managed to get across and shouted, 'I'm free!' That was the signal for the remaining boys to make a concerted rush across, while those in the middle caught as many as possible. When there were more boys in the middle than those left to be caught, the leader shouted, 'Last across', and the game started all over again.

Simple Leap Frog was a favourite mode of progression among small boys. Many a time they steeplechased on their way to school. 'Bab the Bowster', played under a variety of names, was a boisterous game involving ten or twelve boys, one team bending over in a chain with the first boy holding on to a fence or a wall. The other team would then leap upon the bending team's backs, until, after much shaking and heaving, the leaping team fell off. It was called 'Cuddie Lowps', in Aberdeen and Kirkcaldy, where no talking or tickling was allowed; in Edinburgh it was 'Cuddy Hunkers'; in Tarves and Banchory they called it 'Skin the Cuddy'; in Forfar and Dundee, they chanted 'Hucky Duck, three times on and off again'; it was 'Hunch, Cuddy, Hunch' in Stirling, but in Ayrshire they called it 'Bung the Barrel', and in Colston it was simply 'Weight'.

The basic idea in all cases was that the boys in one team all leaned down with their heads down, to make a long cuddy. The front boy was steadied by a boy who stood with his back to a wall, and all the boys in the other team leaped one by one on to the leaning backs, and stayed there, doing their best to make the cuddy collapse. The Cuddy won if the boys could hold out to the count of ten, resisting all attempts to cause their collapse.

In Tarves, one boy at a time had to work his way along the line, his aim being to remove the cap, or touch the head of the Cuddy, i.e. the boy who stood at the front and made a pillar for the rest. The Cuddy heaved about continually, and gave him a rough time, and he was unpopular if, in spite of everything, he managed to reach the front, and was entitled to have another go. On the whole, no matter what its name, it was a tough game, and why there were no serious injuries seems, in retrospect, amazing.

On fine days in the playground, two teams of boys and girls used to play a game called 'Romans and Britons', or 'Rovers and British Soldiers'. They faced each other in two lines, advancing and retiring, one team first singing to the tune of 'Nuts and May'

> Have you any Bread and Wine?
> We are the Rovers.
> Have you any Bread and Wine,
> For we're the gallant sojers.

The second team replied:

> Yes, we have some Bread and Wine,

and claimed that *they* were the Rovers and gallant sojers. A glass of wine was demanded and refused; one team threatened to send for the Red Coats; the second retaliated by a threat to send for the Blue Coats. Both teams then sang, 'Buckle up your sleeves, and we'll have a fight', and a mock battle ensued.

When the teams represented Romans and Britons the procedure was the same.

There was another version supplied by Charlotte, which ran

> Have you any Bread and Wine,
> My siree and my soree?
> Yes, we have some Bread and Wine,
> My siree and my soree.

Having asked for a glass of wine and been refused, the Blue Coats were summoned and the game ended in a fight. In all versions the last question was always, 'Are you ready for a fight?' The reply was 'Yes' and 'battle commenced'.

In describing a game called 'Scots and English' which used to be played in a Fife playground, Alison, in parenthesis remarks, 'We usually had "words" before we started as none of us wanted to be English, and of course half of us had to be! The game simply consisted in each side having a pile of small stones, representing treasure, and the object of the contest was to fight, dodge and scramble our way across to the enemy's side to collect treasure for one's own side – a simple game, yet we got a great deal of enjoyment out of it.'

Emily declares that at her local school boys and girls seldom mixed at games. There was one exception. It was called 'Bedlam', or in the language of the district, 'Bejulam'. Once in a while this chant would go round the playground and the aim was simply for boys of all ages to pursue and catch girls of all ages, and round them up – and that was that! It was a large playground with many boys and girls and it took most of a playtime to do the rounding up.

A game in which both girls and boys joined was called 'Faggots'. The players formed two circles, one within the other, so that the faggots were standing in inward-facing pairs. There was plenty of space between the pairs to allow for chasing. One pair was chosen to be hound and hare – the hound pursuing the hare who took refuge behind one of the pairs of faggots. Immediately this happened the front faggot had to set off, and again the only means of escape was to get behind one of the pairs. If the hound caught a hare the positions were reversed. In Dunfermline this game was known as 'Twos and Threes'.

Sheila remembers how in Ballater School Playground 'during those freezing eleven o'clock breaks in winter weather, we devised this fine way to keep warm. Five or six girls would form a circle, arms linked across each other's shoulders, and in this really close formation we would jump with feet together, stotting round and round chanting

Dirdy coggie, dirdy coggie, dird, dird, dird!

We certainly worked up some heat!'

Andrew tells us that here and there in children's games in Shetland there appear traces of an older time. Boys preferred team games with plenty of hard knocks. Football was played in a very simple way. The ball was thrown down the middle of the field between two teams. The object was to carry, throw, kick or convey in any way the ball to their opponents' end of the field. A swine bladder carefully dried and prepared was used as the inner tube of a leather ball, and was inflated by means of the hollow end of a goose feather. Battles with lumps of turf as missiles in summer, and snowballs in winter were popular, the names of the factions being selected with reference to the prevailing antagonisms of the times, Swedes *v.* Trawlers, Boers *v.* British, and so on.

'Pulling the Baton' was a favourite Shetland game among bigger boys. Two boys sat facing each other, knees drawn up and soles of feet pressing against the opponent's soles. One boy grasped the baton, a short, round stick, in the middle, both hands close together. The other boy grasped the stick with a hand on either side of his opponent's hands. They pulled and tried to raise each other from the sitting position.

Less strenuous was the game called 'Highland Thief'. One boy sat with a number of small stones spread out in front of him, and held a piece of rope or a docken stalk in his hand. A second boy, representing the Highland Thief, approached him and addressed him in these words:

> I come fae da Hielands tidda Lowlands,
> Seekin' geese, gazeleen, an' swine,
> Me peerie salie pawty is run awa'
> An' I warran' he's no amang dine?

which means, 'My little pet piggie has run away, and I feel almost certain he's not among yours?' The seated boy having assured him that it is not among his, invited the second boy to inspect his stock. The Highland Thief carefully examined each pebble, then darted away with one in his hand when he thought he had diverted the owner's attention. If the owner could lash out with his rope and touch the thief before he escaped he had to replace the pebble and try again; but if he got clean away the players changed places.

'King Conelay' was a splendid game for a large number of players. One boy stood in the middle of the field, and at a given word all the others ran from one end of the field to the other. The one in the middle tried to 'pickie', or touch, one of them as they dashed past. The one he managed to touch became his partner to help to touch others as they came streaming back again. As more and more players were picked the catchers had to hold on to their captives long enough to crown them, that is, to tap them three times on the head before they reached the safety of the 'doors' at the far end of the field. The number of catchers went on increasing, finally, the last survivor, who was usually the fastest runner, was caught and crowned King Conelay. Andrew says it is possible that this game may have been founded on remembrance of the days when a man condemned to death was given a last chance of escape if he could race through the crowd of ghoulish spectators and reach safety through the doors of the sanctuary.

'A game we used to play', according to a friend in Argyll, 'seems to have died out as we never see it now. It was called 'Bunnets', the Scots word for bonnets. The playground was divided in two by drawing a foot along the ground to make a dividing line. Then an equal number of boys' caps and girls' berets (or tammies) was laid along opposite ends of the "field". The object of the game was for one side to steal the others bonnets. While you were over on the enemy's side you could be captured by being touched on the top of your head. Then one of your own side had to rescue you by the same practice on the enemy – in both cases it had to be a tap on the top of your head. The game ended when one side had captured all the bunnets. It was most exciting!'

Singing Games

Here we go round the Jingo Ring
About the Merry-ma-Tanzie.

Though many modern playground games tend to be based on what is seen on television, and there are a number of innovations, especially among skipping rhymes, it is encouraging to find that a good number of the old singing games which seem to have been played almost exclusively by girls, are being handed down from one generation to the next, both in town and countryside. Dundee, I am informed, is doing something practical to preserve them. Attractive cards have been designed, illustrating how the old games used to be played, and giving the words of once-popular bairn-rhymes.

Secondary school-girls who heard a tape-recording of playground games collected some years ago were really interested and excited, and kept remembering games and songs from primary school days. In February 1973, the girls were planning, with a member of Dundee Museum Staff, to make a film of Dundee songs and dances.

Of the large number of singing games which have been handed on by an endless chain of bairns, some are said to be derived from customs of great antiquity. There were some in which, without knowing it, bairns were probably joining in a pagan ritual in honour of the Goddess of Spring; when they sang:

Here we come gathering Nuts in May
On a cold and frosty morning,

Singing games

they were unaware that the two Sides lined up facing each other may have been a relic of the days when two families met to discuss the coming marriage of two of their members; they might even have been enacting a marriage by capture. Bairns have never been known to query the assumption that nuts could be gathered in May; even the theory that it should be sung 'Nuts and May' or 'Knots of May' (knots being an old name for posies or little knots of flowers) hardly explains that cold and frosty morning. More feasible is the interpretation of the rhyme as a chain of events in the seasons of the year – Spring with mayflowers, Autumn with ripe nuts, Winter with cold and frosty mornings.

Some games mentioned in these pages, recollected by those who played them, have now disappeared, and some, naturally, have changed over the years. Many of them had appropriate accompaniments, and when gracefully and quietly carried out by young performers were very pretty and picturesque. Perhaps music is the most evocative factor when it comes to reviving memories of the days of auld lang syne, and among these musical memories are the old melodies for singing games that were part dance.

There is 'The Grand Old Duke of York', for example, and 'The Jolly Miller'. These almost achieved the status of Country Dances, for they were often performed indoors by adults, as well as by children in the playground.

The following children's riddle, which appears in the *Scottish National Dictionary*, is one of several variants, and the reason for its inclusion here will presently be made apparent:

> As I went up by Humber Jumber,
> Humber Jumber, Jeinie O,
> There I met Sir Hoker Poker
> Carrying away Campeinie, O.
> If I had had my tit-my-tat,
> My tit-my-tat, my teinie, O,
> I'd never have let Sir Hoker Poker
> Carry away Campeinie, O!

The answer to the riddle is 'wolf, lamb and shepherd'; a tit-my-tat, suggesting the sound of a shot, was the name given in riddles to a gun. In recent years, Miss Jean C. Milligan, of Scottish Country Dancing fame, set the words of the riddle to the music of an original Scottish Country Dance, which her pupils sang as they danced. Her version, according to Margaret, her pupil and fellow-enthusiast, was slightly different from the above lines, using Jeilie and Teilie instead of Jeinie and Teinie, and the last two lines being

> I'd have made Sir Hoker Poker
> Lay down Campeillie, O!

'Babbity Bowster' used to be danced by children in Glasgow. 'Wha learned you tae dance?', they asked,

> Babbity, Bowster, Babbity Bowster,
> Wha learned you tae dance, Babbity Bowster, brawly?

And the reply came

> My minnie learned me tae dance, Babbity Bowster,
> Babbity Bowster,
> My minnie learned me tae dance, Babbity Bowster, brawly.

The next question was

An' wha gied you the keys tae keep, Babbity Bowster?

and the answer, as before, was

My minnie gied me the keys tae keep, Babbity Bowster, brawly.

Another version went like this:

> Bea-ba-babbity, babbity, babbity,
> Bea-ba-babbity, Bab-at-the-Bowster, brawly.

If the boys could be persuaded to join in the game, they all joined hands and romped round a boy in the centre, who was commanded to

Kneel down on the ground, on the ground, on the ground,
Kneel down on the ground and kiss the bonnie wee lassie.

He then spread a handkerchief (originally it was a bolster, hence 'bowster') and knelt in front of his chosen partner, they kissed and danced off together. When a girl was chosen to be in the centre, she declared emphatically

I'd raither hae a bonnie wee laddie!

'My first introduction to Bea-ba-babbity was at a Glasgow University Graduation ceremony', Elsie reflects. 'The Chancellor's name was Finlayson, and as each girl graduate came forward to be 'capped', the students in the gallery sang with great enthusiasm,

> Heigh Ho, Finlayson,
> Kiss the bonnie wee lassie!

'Babbity Bowster' and 'Bab-at-the-Bowster' must not be confused with 'Bab the Bowster,' which is a strenuous form of Leap Frog. 'Babbity Bowster' was a popular game among adults as well as children. At one time it was chosen to finish all wedding-parties which were held in the barn or village school. The girls sat on one side of the barn, the lads on the other. There was ample opportunity for kissing-in-the-ring with all those bonnie wee lassies kneeling on a handkerchief and choosing partners with whom to scamper right out of sight.

'The Village Green' is an original game which was composed some years ago by Margaret, an Edinburgh teacher, for her five-year-old pupils who were taking part in a May Queen Fête. Later, they performed it at a Musical Festival and won a Banner: the words are:

> Will you come and dance with me
> Upon the Village Green,
> All the boys and girls will come
> To choose who will be Queen.
> We'll point our toes and clap our hands
> And dance round in a ring,
> I would like to be the Queen
> If you will be the King,
> Tra la la la.

The appropriate actions were set to a tune with a Scottish flavour.

A dancing game remembered by Caroline was played by small girls moving round singing to one in the centre:

> A little girl I know a-dancing did go
> Boom-far-a-la, boom-far-a-la, boom-far-a-la-lee!
> And if there should be a partner for me,
> Boom-far-a-la, boom-far-a-la, boom-far-a-la-lee!
> Take my hand and dance along with me,
> Boom-far-a-la, boom-far-a-la, boom-far-a-la-lee!

A partner having been chosen the two danced in the ring together, while the others boom-far-a-la'd. The partner then took her place in the centre and the game continued till every girl had taken part in the dance.

> We are jolly sailor boys
> Just newly come ashore,
> We'll spend our time in drinking wine
> As we have done before.

In this game two girls linked arms and skipped round the outside of a ring formed by the others. When these 'two jolly sailor boys' had introduced themselves in the above words, the other girls promised that:

> They shall have a round and a ring,
> They shall have a pretty pretty girl
> For to dance upon the shore.

A second couple was chosen to dance with them, and this went on till all were dancing, and the long tail of dancers waltzed all round the playground.

This song, 'Katie Bairdie' has been sung within living memory in a great many parts of Scotland. It goes back hundreds of years and is mentioned by Scott in *The Fortunes of Nigel*. Sir Walter knew it as a dance tune. Katie began her life as Katherine Beardie in the early seventeenth century. Down the years her name has changed innumerable times and, among others, it appears as Katie Beardie, Kitty Bairdie, and Katie Bairdie. She is remembered chiefly for her coo and other livestock.

> Katie Bairdie hid a coo,
> Black an' white aboot the mou'
> Wasna that a dentie coo?
> Dance, Katie Bairdie!
>
> Katie Bairdie hid a hen,
> Cackled but an' cackled ben,
> Wasna that a dentie hen?
> Dance, Katie Bairdie!
>
> Katie Bairdie hid a cock
> That could spin backin' rock.
> Wasna that a dentie cock?
> Dance, Katie Bairdie!
>
> Katie Bairdie hid a cat,
> She could catch baith moose an' rat.
> Wasna that a dentie cat?
> Dance, Katie Bairdie!
>
> Katie Bairdie hid a grice,
> It could skate upon the ice.
> Wasna that a dentie grice?
> Dance, Katie Bairdie!

If more verses were needed for skipping, the following were added:

> Katie Bairdie hid a wife,
> She could use baith fork an' knife,
> Wasna that a dentie wife?
> Dance, Katie Bairdie!

104

Katie Bairdie hid a wean
Wadna play when it cam' on rain!
Wasna that a dentie wean?
Dance, Katie Bairdie!

Katie Bairdie hid a coo,
It was yellow, black, an' blue,
A' the monkeys i' the Zoo
Lauched at Katie Bairdie's coo!

A game that has been known for generations and is still popular among girls is 'The Dusty Bluebells', known variously as The Dusting, Saucy, or Fairy Bluebells. This is how it was played in Auchterarder: The girls stood in a ring with hands joined and held high to make archways. One girl stood in the centre and when the singing began, she went round the ring, passing in and out of the arches. The words were:

In and out the Dusty Bluebells,
In and out the Dusty Bluebells,
In and out the Dusty Bluebells,
I am your master.

The second verse ran:

Pitter Patter on your shoulder
Pitter Patter on your shoulder
Pitter Patter on your shoulder,
I am your master!

While that was being sung, she stood behind one of the girls and pitter-pattered with her fingers on the other girl's shoulder. The two girls then went in and out the Dusty Bluebells, and pitter-pattered on the shoulders of a third girl who joined them; thus the game that began in a ring ended in a long train which the last girl led here and there around the playground, till the supposed train came to a station and somebody said 'Stop!'

In another version the words and actions Tuppy Tappy were used instead of Pitter Patter, and the game was called 'The Dusky Bluebells'.

'The Bluebird' was danced by small children in Edinburgh.

The ring formation was as for 'The Dusty Bluebells', with one child going in and out of the arches, stopping in front of another child who joined hands and hopped and danced with her, and then became The Bluebird in her turn. The game went on till all the children had been Bluebirds. The words were:

> Here comes a Bluebird through my window,
> Hi diddle I dum di,
> Take a little hop and dance in the corner,
> Take a little hop and dance with me,
> Take a little hop and dance in the corner,
> Hi diddle I dum di.

There was also the well-known game of 'The Gallant Ship', beloved of littlins in Torrance and other districts, who romped around singing:

> Three times round went the galley galley ship,
> And three times round went she,
> Three times round went the galley galley ship
> And she sank to the bottom of the sea.

They crouched while they sang,

> Pull-er-up, pull-er-up, sang the jolly sailor boy,
> As she sank to the bottom of the sea.

The next verse went,

> No, I won't, No, I won't, sang the jolly sailor boy.

But when he sang,

> Yes, I will, Yes, I will

they all bounced happily to their feet.

Strathmiglo bairns sang:

> The Good Ship sails through the ally ally O,
> The ally ally O, the ally ally O,
> The Good Ship sails through the ally ally O,
> On the fourteenth of September.

This was followed by,

> Try, try and sink her,
> On the fourteenth of September.

While singing, all the children passed under an arch made by
one girl who held her arms fully outstretched with her hands
resting on a wall. When she brought her arms down and
caught somebody it was that girl's turn to stand at the wall.

As will be seen, many of the oldest singing games are
founded on Love, Courtship, Marriage and Death, which
children associated with everyday life. In the following, as in
others, it is bluntly stated:

> All she wants is a nice young man.

The game begins with:

> There stands a lady on the mountain,
> Who she is I do not know,
> All she wants is gold and silver,
> All she wants is a nice young man.

Which long since has been promoted to the ballad status of 'O,
No, John'. Having got her nice young man she sometimes lost
him, as in this game, where the girl sings,

> Broken-hearted I wandered at the loss of my beloved,
> He was a jolly sailor before he went away,
> He had a silver sixpence, and he broke it in two
> And to me he gave the one half before he went away.

Charlotte contributes an old Scots courtship song with a
pastoral flavour:

> Queen Mary, Queen Mary, my age is sixteen,
> My faither's a fermer on yon village green,
> He has plenty o' siller tae dress me sae braw,
> But there's nae bonnie laddie tae tak' me awa'.

One girl now faced the others who had been advancing and
retiring. She sings,

> One morning I rose and I looked in the glass,
> Says I tae masel', 'I'm a handsome young lass'.

She chose one from the line and they stood facing each other:

> Put my hands on my sides, and I gave a 'Ha! Ha!',
> There's nae bonnie laddie tae tak' me awa'.

The girls changed places, and the singing continued till every girl had had her turn to choose another.

Similar words are used in other games as will be noticed.

'Here are two dancing and singing games we used to play in the sheds at school', says Emily. 'We stood on the long bench at the back except one girl who stood in front and sang:

> Red apples, red apples, by night and by day
> I love sweet Betty and Betty loves me.

Betty then joined the girl in front, they clasped hands and danced round while the others sang:

> I wash her in milk and I dry her with silk
> I write down her name with a gold pen and ink.
> One morning I rose and I looked in the glass
> And I said to myself, 'What a handsome young lass!'
> My hands by my side and I gave a Ha Ha,
> There's nae bonnie laddie tae tak' me awa'!

Betty then took her place in front and chose another girl, and the game went on till every girl had been chosen.

Surnames of the actual players were used in the second song which began

> Mrs Johnstone lives ashore
> With a knocker on her door,
> When a sailor comes ashore
> He knocks at Mrs Johnstone's door.

The girl with the surname Johnstone joined the girl in front, who was presumably the sailor, and they swung round together while the other girls sang

> Alla balla alla balla bee,
> Alla balla A B C,
> Alla balla alla balla bee
> Married to a sailor.

A pretty game which I remember playing very often in GlenGairn was based on the story of the Sleeping Beauty. We sang

> Briar Rosebud was a bonny lass
> Long long ago.

and went on to tell how she was visited by an Ugly Fairy who gave her a rose; on its thorn she pricked her finger, and fell asleep for a hundred years. The briars grew thick around her lonely tower, till Prince Charming came by and cut them down. The final verse declared that 'Briar Rosebud was a happy bride'. All through this singing game the refrain was 'Long Long ago'.

Weeping for a sweetheart was a favourite theme:

> I'm a little Sandy Girl
> Sitting on a stone,
> Crying and weeping all the day alone.
> Stand up, Sandy Girl, wipe your tears away,
> Choose the one you love the best
> And then run away.

Sometimes this was sung as 'Sandy Boy' to give the boys a turn.

Another for the boys was

> Little Alexander sitting on the grass,
> Weeping and wailing for a nice young lass
> Rise up, Sandy, wipe away your tears,
> Here's the bonnie lassie that you love so dear.

Sometimes the words were:

> Little Sally Walker sitting in the sun
> Weeping and crying for a young man,
> Rise, Sally Walker, wipe your tears away,
> Choose to the East, choose to the West,
> Choose to the very one that you love the best.

or:

> Little Sally Waters sitting in the sun
> Roarin' an' greetin' for a young man,
> Rise, Sally Waters, wipe away your tears,
> Choose to the East, choose to the West,
> Choose to the very ane that you love the best.

But of all the versions,

> Poor Nellie [Mary or Jenny] is a-weeping
> On a bright summer's day,

109

was by a long way the favourite, though all were played in the same way. Any number of girls could take part in the game which was played in a ring, with one girl kneeling in the centre with her hands to her face and apparently weeping. The others moved round singing. The second verse asked:

> What is Nellie weeping for
> On a bright summer's day.

And the answer was

> She's weeping for a sweetheart
> On a bright summer's day.

Nellie was invited to stand up and

> Choose the one you love the best,
> Choose once, choose twice,
> Choose her three times over.

Then came the Marriage Blessing:

> Now you are married we wish you joy,
> First a girl and then a boy,
> Seven years after, a son and a daughter,
> Pray, young couple, come kiss together,
> Kiss her once, kiss her twice,
> Kiss her three times over.

The two in the ring gave each other a boisterous embrace, while the others ran round them very rapidly.

It is possible that ring games go back to the time when there used to be a gathering of representatives of both families to arrange a marriage, hence the advice to the young couple that often followed:

> Now that you two are married thegither,
> You must obey your faither an' mither,
> An' love ane anither like sister an' brither,
> Now, young couple come kiss thegither.

'Round and round the Village' is a very old traditional game which is based on village festivals at which marriages took place. It was the custom for the young people to go through the houses in procession. In the game the children made arches

with their hands held high and all had a turn at weaving in and
out of the arches and repeating

> In and out the windows,
> As we have done before.

Then came the instruction

> Stand and face your lover
> As you have done before,

followed in some places by 'Follow her to London', but more
commonly by

> Try, try and catch her
> As you have done before,

ending in a capture, and the Marriage Blessing,

> Now you are married we wish you joy,
> First a girl and then a boy.

Another ring game with courtship in view has survived in
various forms to the present day. It begins with all singing in a
moving ring, with one girl in the middle:

> The wind, the wind, the wind blows high,
> The snow comes falling from the sky,

or:

> Rain, rain high, the wind doth blow,
> The clouds are gathering to and fro,

or:

> The rain comes pattering [or scattering, or blattering]
> from the sky,

The verse goes on:

> [Mary Thomson] says she'll die
> If she doesn't get a fellow with a roving eye [or
> a rolling eye].

Today, in Edinburgh, they sing:

> If she doesn't get a fellow with a rainbow tie!

111

The lines that follow may be:

> He is handsome, she is pretty
> She is the girl of the Golden City,

or:

> she is the girl of the Highland City

or:

> she is the Belle of New York City.

Then the verse continues:

> She has lovers, one, two, three,
> Please will you tell me who they be.
> [Johnnie Smith] says he'll have her,
> All the lads are fighting for her,
> Let the lads say what they will,
> Johnnie Smith has her still;
> Johnnie Smith's a nice young man,
> He comes to the door with his hat in his hand,
> Down comes she, all dressed in silk,
> A rose in her bosom as white as milk,
> She takes off her glove and shows me the ring,
> Tomorrow, tomorrow the wedding will begin.

Or:

> Out she comes as white as snow,
> With rings on her fingers and bells on each toe,
> And says to her lover, with a sigh,
> 'I'm in love with a fellow with a roving eye'.

As in most courtship songs, she gets her lover in the end. Every district has its own version; the surprising thing is that the game has survived so long, and covers such a wide area.

Children who live in an Edinburgh housing estate performed it at a musical festival, as part of an exhibition of Old Edinburgh in the Waverley Market. They followed the words 'Please can you tell me' with a confidential

> A is his first name,
>   E-I-O!
> B is his second name.
>   E-I-O!
> Andrew Brown is his name.
>   E-I-O!

This is a Glasgow singing game:

> Down in yonder valley [or meadow] where the green grass
> grows,
> There [Lucy Locket] bleaches her clothes,
> She sang, she sang, she sang so sweet
> She sang of [Tommy Piper] across the street.
> He hugged her, he kissed her, he took her on his knee,
> And said, Dear Lucy, I hope we will agree.

In 1886, William, then a boy of five, sang it in Dreghorn, and
still remembers how it continues:

> He hugged her, he kissed her, he bought her a gown,
> A gown, a gown, a guinea-gold gown,
> He bought her a hat with a feather at the back,
> A pea-brown cherry on a pea-brown hat.
> She went down to the draper's at the corner of the street
> To buy a pair of blankets and a pair of sheets,
> And half-a-yard of moleskin
> To mend Willie's breeks!

In the same year they sang in Dreghorn:

> Queen Anne, Queen Anne sits in her sedan,
> Fair as a lily, white as a swan,
> A pair of white gloves are over her hands
> And she is the fairest in all the land.
> Buy my lilies, buy my roses,
> Make them into pretty posies
> For the maiden you will choose.

Other children sang of a pair of *green* gloves, and went on:

> Come taste my lilies, come smell my roses.

'Three Dukes from Spain' was a courtship game,
sometimes known as 'The Three Knights'. Three girls stood
facing a line formed by the others, and sang:

> There were three knights who came from Spain
> To call upon my sister Jane;
> My sister Jane is far too young,
> She cannot bear a flattering tongue,
> So I'll away, and I'll away,
> And call again another day.

The girls in the line replied,

> Come back, come back, your coach is free,
> And choose the bonniest one you see.

The first knight then declared:

> The bonniest one that I can see
> Is bonnie wee [Mary] will you come with me?

The second and third knights each named a girl, who stepped out of the line and all three took the place of the knights, and so the game went on.

Another game with its origin in marriage customs, was sung in a moving ring:

> Here we go round the Jingo Ring
> About the Merry-ma-Tanzie.

The theme is universally known, but the origin is obscure. 'Mit mir tanzen' (literally 'dance with me') suggests that it may be of German origin. Children in every part of Scotland have danced it for generations. The verse continued:

> Here's a bride just new come hame
> About the Merry-ma-Tanzie.

They sang her Christian name, her surname, and her lover's names, and finally sang:

> Tell the bride to hide her face,

which she did, then chose another girl to play the part of the bride, and they changed places.

Right through the sunny summer days in Glen Gairn we 'Dropped the Handkerchief' sitting on the grass in a wide circle.

Two girls were involved at a time – the one who dawdled outside the circle and the one behind whose back the handkerchief was dropped. The first strolled round chanting,

> I sent a letter to my love,
> And by the way I dropped it,
> I dree, I dree, I dropped it.

> One of you has picked it up
> And put it in your pocket.
> It wasn't YOU, It wasn't YOU
> It was YOU!

She then ran round the ring as fast as she could, the other giving chase.

Henry recounts occasions 'when we were at Kingswells before the 1914 War, my mother used to invite the Bethany children from Aberdeen for a sort of glorified picnic. They played

> I sent a letter to my Love
> And by the way I dropped it,
> An auld man picked it up
> And put it in his pocket,
> P-O-C-K-E-T, pocket

'Then they ran round singing "The doggie winna bite YOU, nor YOU, nor YOU (ad lib, and molto accelerando) but YOU", which was followed by a chase.'

Sometimes the words, 'I wrote a letter to my Love' were preceded by 'Itiskit, itaskit, a green and yellow basket', and in Leven, the words were:

> Itiskit, itaskit, I had a little basket,
> I went out to the shop one day
> And I lost it by the way.
> Look up to the skies, and blind your eyes,
> And never look behind you.

In Rosehearty, the game was called 'Black Doggie', and the girl behind whose back the handkerchief was dropped was OUT if she did not notice it before her neighbours in the circle did.

'Oats, Peas, Beans and Barley' is a game as old as Time. In Dunfermline this version was played:

> Oats, peas, beans and barley grow [repeat]
> Do you or I or anyone know
> How oats, peas, beans and barley grow?
> First, the farmer sows his seed,
> Then he stands and takes his ease,
> Stamps his feet, and claps his hand,
> And turns around and views his land.

This was followed by 'waiting for a partner', which is interesting, because choosing a partner indicated the custom of courtship and marriage after the Spring Festival. Finally, they sang:

> Now you are married you must obey,
> You must be true in all you say,
> You must be kind, you must be good,
> And keep your wife in kindling-wood.

This courtship song used to be sung in the streets of Glasgow.

> O, I'll gie you a dress o' reid
> A' stitched roon wi' silver threid,
> Gin ye will marry-arry-arry-arry,
> Gin ye will marry me.
>> (The girl declines his dress o'
>> reid, and says she will *not*
>> marry-arry him.)

He then promises:

> I'll gie you a silver spoon
> Tae feed the wean in the efternune
> If you will marry-arry-arry-arry,
> If you will marry me.
>> (Again she declines his offer.)

Next he offers:

> I'll gie you the keys o' ma chest,
> An' a' the money that I possess,
> Gin ye will marry-arry-arry-arry,
> Gin ye will marry me.'
>> (With alacrity she accepts)
> O yes, I'll tak' the keys o' yer chest,
> An' a' the money that ye possess,
> An' I will marry-arry-arry-arry,
> I will marry you!

To this he replies:

> Eh, guidsakes, ye're awfy funny,
> Ye dinna love *me*, but ye love ma money,
> An' I'll no marry-arry-arry-arry,
> I'll no' marry YOU!

Another courtship game was played by two lines of girls facing each other, advancing and retiring. The first line of girls sang:

> Coming up the seashore, seashore, seashore,
> Coming up the seashore, E-I-O.
> We want to marry, marry, marry,
> We want to marry, E-I-O.

The second line, representing potential suitors, sang

> Marry one of us–a, us–a, us–a,
> Marry one of us–a, E-I-O.

But the girls turned their backs on them, wiping their feet ostentatiously and singing,

> You're all too dirty, dirty, dirty,
> You're all too dirty, E-I-O.

In Forfar they rejected suitors in these words,

> I wudna hae a baker ava,
> I wudna hae a baker ava,
> For he sits an' he cracks,
> An' he burns a' his baps,
> An' I wudna hae a baker ava!

> I wudna hae a weaver ava,
> I wudna hae a weaver ava,
> For he sits an' he girns,
> An' he raivels his pirns,
> An' I wudna hae a weaver ava!

Here is one of the oldest and best-known traditional singing games, possibly with its origin in a marriage dance round a sacred tree or bush:

> Here we go round the Mulberry Bush, the Mulberry Bush, the Mulberry Bush,
> Here we go round the Mulberry Bush on a cold and frosty morning.

After singing the first verse while moving round in a ring with hands joined, the children used to follow the actions of washing, ironing, mending, etc., singing:

> This is the way we wash our clothes
> On a cold and frosty morning.

The final verse, which was 'This is the way we lace our stays', has long been obsolete!

There are a number of old games which contain the words 'This is the way'; Margaret reminds us of the one called 'Visiting' of which we have already heard, in which the children sang:

> I went to visit friends one day
> They only lived across the way,
> They said they couldn't come out to play
> Because it was their washing day.
> This is the way we wash all day, wash all day,
>   wash all day,
> This is the way we wash all day
> Because it is the washing-day.

This was followed by ironing, sweeping, dusting, cooking and playing, all with appropriate actions. And there was the familiar

> When I was a lady, I went this way and that,

followed by:

> When I was a teacher, I went this way and that,

then

> When I got married, I went this way and that,

and

> When I had a baby I went this way and that.

More marriage prospects are contained in this one:

> Jack-a-needle, Jack-a-needle, I sew with my needle,
> And when I get married how happy I'll be,
> I'll go to my garden and sit there all morning,
> And whistle on [Johnnie] to come unto me.

On a sombre note is 'London Bridge is falling down', a very old game which is supposed to have originated in the ancient custom of making a foundation-sacrifice at the building of a bridge, namely a Fair Lady. It was sung for years as 'Broken Bridges falling down', but the present generation has reverted to the orthodox 'London Bridge' as this is now a familiar place, many of the children having been there on school excursions.

The old way of playing the game was to catch a prisoner, swing her back and forth, and before setting her free to demand a guinea-gold ring. If this was not forthcoming, 'Off to prison she must go, My Fair Lady!' She was then taken aside and asked to choose an apple or a pear. When all had chosen, the two sides had a tug of war.

A singing game which gave every girl a turn to be in the centre of the ring was:

> Water, water, wallflowers, growing up so high,
> We are all maidens and we must all die,
> Except [Nellie Ritchie] the youngest of us all,
> She can hop and she can skip
> And she can turn her mangle-stick,
> Fie, Fie, Fie for shame!
> Turn your back to the wall again!

Thus it was sung in Ballater, but in Burghead it was said of 'the youngest of us all':

> She can dance and she can sing,
> And she can do the Highland Fling.
> Fly, fly, fly for shame,
> Turn your back and look again!

In Shetland, they sang 'Water, Water, Wildflower' and they were 'all ladies and they must all die', except the youngest who was told to turn her face to the wall again. In course of time they were all facing the other way, which ended the game.

In Leven they sang:

> Water, water, wallflowers, growing up so high,
> All the little daisies have all got to die,
> Except little Nancy, she's the only one,

> She can dance and she can sing
> And she can dance the Highland Fling.

In another version the:

> youngest flower can dance and sing
> and she can knock the wall ower.

Or

> She can knock you all ower.

In Strathmiglo, over fifty-five years ago, they sang:

> Watery, watery, wallflowers, growing up so high,
> We are all maidens and we've all got to die,
> Except the youngest daughter,

and at the words 'Turn your back to the wall again', all turned, and the girl in the middle made her escape, to be replaced by the one who let her through.

Elizabeth produced this lament which was apparently addressed to a man who had been given a sentence of Sixty Days. It came from Leven and was played like 'Water, Water, Wallflowers'. It must originally have been sung in the vicinity of a prison, but where the prison was situated was not revealed:

> There stands a prison, a very high prison,
> The windows are peerin' tae the sky,
> The lassies they are greetin',
> The ladies they are weepin',
> Cheer up! Cheer up! I'll see you by-and-bye!
> So come along, Mary, my bonnie bonnie Mary,
> Ye'll have tae stand this weepin' sixty days,
> The sixty days are comin',
> They'll no' be very long,
> Cheer up! Cheer up!
> We'll meet you by-and-bye!

An unusual game played in Shetland appeared to have had its origin in some forgotten folk-lore. The chief characters in it were the Midder and Janey Jo. The Midder sat in the middle of a ring of girls, all with lowered heads and eyes on the ground. At the outset, a scraping noise was heard, made by the girl

120

who was out of sight of the others, and they cried out in fear, 'Oh Midder, what's yon?' and she replied, soothingly, 'It's naethin', just the dog scrapin' at the door.' Next a moan was heard, and all the children cried, 'Oh, Midder, what's yon?' and her reply was 'Just the wind in the lum.' Then came a shuffling noise – again the cry was 'What's yon?' and the Midder's answer was 'It's naethin' but the cow in the byre.' So the game went on with more strange noises, the children asking in great agitation, 'What's yon?' and the Midder producing a satisfactory explanation for each one. Finally, she raised her head, noticed that the hitherto unseen player had entered and was standing near her, and in a voice of horror, she exclaimed, 'It's Janey Jo risen from the dead!' The children shrieked and scattered, pursued by Janey Joe. The child who was caught was the next to 'rise from the dead.' This could be a thrilling game if the Midder and Janey Jo were good at acting, and could sustain the eeriness and tense excitement.

There are many other games which are associated with the subject of death and burial. One of the best-remembered began as a courting song, and ended in the death of a girl who was known as Georgina in all the fishing villages along the Banffshire coast before the First World War. She was Janny Jo in Angus, Janey Jo in Shetland, Janet Jo in Edinburgh and the Stewartry of Kirkcudbright, and simply Poor Jenny in Aberdeenshire. She has even been called Jenny Jones, but in error. It ought to be Jenny Jo, the old Scots word for sweetheart, as in 'John Anderson, my Jo.'

The game might have been gloomy in GlenGairn had we not sung it so light-heartedly. It went on, and on, and on, about a sadly-overworked Jenny. It began:

> We've come to see poor Jenny
> An' hoo's she the day?

The answer was,

> She's up the stairs washin'
> An' ye can't see her the day.

A succession of duties, such as ironing and baking kept her in the background till at last she was said to be up the stairs dead, or dying, 'and you can't see her the day'. But that was not the end. The next problem was 'What shall we wear at the funeral?'

> White is for weddings, and that will not do,
> Blue is for sailors and that will not do,

nor will red, which is for soldiers, but

> Black is for mourning and so that will do.

In Sandend and other places they gave no thought to what they would wear at the funeral, but were much concerned about what they would dress Georgina in. Blue is for sailors, red is for soldiers, black is for mourning – none of these would do. Finally, the question, 'What shall we dress her in?' was satisfactorily settled, for

> White is for angels, and so that will do.

In the Stewartry version, the mother admitted that:

> Janet Jo is dead an' gane, dead an' gane,
> She'll never come hame,

so Janet Jo was carried away to be buried, all following the weeping lover; but she was sometimes revived just in time. Children who played games involving death preferred the dead person to come to life again, so if Janet Joe decided to be revived all were satisfied.

In Angus, Janny Jo had evidently been on the sick list, and her mother, as in all other versions, was there to answer kind inquiries.

> We've come tae speir for Janny Jo,
> An' hoo's she the day?

If Janny Jo had slept well and eaten a good breakfast, the inquirers sang 'Good Luck to Janny Jo', but if Janny Jo was far from well, the chant was 'Bad Luck for Janny Jo'.

When her mother admitted she was dead, the question of 'What will we dress her in' became paramount. As in other places, they decided, 'White is for angels, and so that will do.' Janny Jo was carried off to her grave, but on the way recovered consciousness, and chased the mourners, who fled with shrieks of delight. The first to be caught became the next Janny Joe.

A doleful ditty sung in many places was:

Old Rodger is dead and laid in his grave, Heigh Ho! Laid in
  his grave.
[circling slowly round a boy with his jacket over his head]
They planted an apple tree over his head, Heigh Ho! etc.,
                [all pretend to be digging and planting]
The apples got ripe and they all fell off, Heigh Ho! etc.,
    [raising and lowering hands to indicate apples falling]
There came an old woman [a girl entered the ring] came
  picking them up [everybody began picking them up]
Old Rodger got up and gave her a kick.
[and chased her round the ring, which moved round, giving
                a kick as the words were sung.]

In Glasgow they sang 'The Lodger is dead and laid in his
grave', and it was an old man who came picking up apples; the
Lodger got up and gave him a kick, then tried to catch
someone in the circle, which then broke up as the players ran
away from the Lodger. The first one caught took the Lodger's
place.

Gullane's version was 'Poor Tommy is dead and laid in his
grave', and the game ended with Tommy chasing the old
woman round and round and attempting to kick her. In
Edinburgh they sang 'Poor Tommy is dead, dead in his grave'
and rather heartlessly ended the verse with 'Tra la la'!

In another district they sang 'Old Rodger is dead and lies in
his grave', and gaily ended with a 'Doh, Ray, Me'!

In some schools 'old Rodger is dead and laid in his grave'
was followed by E-I-O which was sung as a long-drawn-out
wail.

There were several games involving widows, always 'poor
widows'. In many places the advancing line sang:

> Here's a poor widow who's left alone,
> She has no body to marry upon,

or:

> Here's a poor widow, she's left alone,
> She has no money to marry upon,

but in Glasgow it was:

> Here's a poor widow from Babylon,
> Wi' six puir bairns a' alane,
> Yin can bake an' yin can brew,
> Yin can shape an' yin can shew [sew]
> Yin can sit at the fire an' spin,
> An' yin can mak a cake for the King,
> Come pick ye East an' pick ye West
> An' pick the yin ye lo'e the best.

In Lanark, the bairns sang with great feeling about the 'poor widow from Sandilands'. Margaret explains that they felt really sad while they were singing, as if they knew the poor widow personally and shared her sorrow at parting from her children. This was probably because the village of Sandilands is situated not far from Lanark. This is the way it was played: one of the big girls took the children by the hand and led them forward, all singing:

> Here's a poor widow from Sandilands
> With all her children by their hands.
> One can knit and one can sew
> And one can make a white lily grow,
> O, please take one in, O please take one in!

one child was picked and went over to the other side. The singing continued:

> And now poor Mary she has gone
> Without a farthing in her hand,
> Nothing but a guinea-gold ring,
> Goodbye, Mary, Goodbye!

At this point, a sensitive child was known to burst into tears.

Elsie writes 'A friend, now aged seventy-nine, tells me that, in her day, games such as "Relieveo" and "Smoogle" were not considered ladylike, but that hand-clapping played a major part in many of the singing-games. A favourite hand-clapping rhyme was

> Mrs Brown went to town
> Riding on a pony,
> When she came back
> She took off her hat
> And called on Mrs Maloney.

Another was

> O what a cold you've got!
> Take me to the doctor's shop,
> Doctor, doctor, will I die?
> Yes, you'll die, and so will I,
> Take one glass
> Of potass,
> That will send your cold away!

It was a recognised chore for some children to run in their dinner-hour with their father's dinner in an enamelled can with a domed lid. I never speculated about the contents of *my* father's dinner-can, but it would certainly not have been what this hand-clapping rhyme declares:

> My mother says I must go
> With my daddy's dinner-O,
> Chappit tatties, beef an' steak,
> Twa red herrings and an oatmeal cake.'

The Burlesque Band was a riotous indoor game. My mother used to sing it, and she taught us how to take part. First we sang:

> O we can play on the Big Bass Drum
> And this is the music to it.

We imitated the Big Bass Drum, and with each succeeding verse another instrument was added: the Bugle, the Double Bass, the Tambourine, the Old Banjo, the Castanets, the Kettledrum, the Flute, and any other instrument that children cared to suggest. When a new instrument was announced the previous ones had to be imitated in their correct order, and 'this is the way we do it' repeated as often as necessary, finishing thus:

> O we can play on the Castanets and this is the
> music to it,
> Tick–ticka–tack is the Castanet
> Tum–a–tum–tum is the Old Banjo,
> Jing–a–jing–jing is the Tambourine,
> Zoo–zoo–zoo is the Double Bass,
> Tan–tan–tarra is the Bugle Horn,
> And rig–jig–boom is the Big Bass Drum
> And this is the way we do it.

Skipping Rhymes

Matthew, Mark, Luke, and John,
Haud the cuddy till I win on,
Haud him fast an' haud him steady,
Haud him like a Finnan Haddie.

Skipping as a form of girls' recreation is said to be as widespread as ever it was, and prevails during the Spring months of the year, the months when seed is springing up, for skipping and swinging are closely connected with the dancing and leaping that usually accompanied pagan rituals relating to the growth of crops.

Skipping began in April, or as soon as snow was off the ground, and continued all Summer, well into Autumn, till the days began to draw in and the weather became cold and wet.

Skipping memories range from a small girl's early efforts at home with her very first, her very own skipping-rope with wooden handles, to a length of tracer-rope ca'd by two girls in the playground, and thereafter to complicated French and German ropes, and the sophisticated routines of skipping to music in a Young Ladies' Dancing Class in Edinburgh.

'Salt, Mustard, Vinegar, Pepper' – thousands of bairns have through the ages blithely skipped to that old chant.

Two girls ca'd the rope, the others in a steady stream ran in, skipped the agreed number of times, and ran out at the other end. To trip was to be OUT. The last girl had to skip on the spot at speed, till she, too, tripped, or was 'tickled' (caused to trip) or gave up for want of puff.

There was the game of 'Bumps' or 'Fireys', when the rope had to pass twice under the skipper's feet while she was still in the air.

An accompanying rhyme from the homely back-streets of Glasgow was

> I love sugar, I love tea,
> I love sitting on a black man's knee,

and from the little fishing-village of Gourdon, calling every girl in turn by name

> House to let, Apply within,
> Let Mary go out and Bella come in.

Tracer-rope was preferred to hairy binder-twine which had not the right weight or substance, but, unfortunately, it soon frayed by constant friction. A crisis was averted when somebody's mother donated a piece of clothes-line, but the bairns were punished if they annexed it without permission. The chant in Leven was

> Wavy, wavy, ca' the rope ower,
> Ane, twa, three, fower,

but in Kinross it was

> Eevie, ivie, ca' the rope ower,

swinging the rope slowly from side to side before turning it, gradually increasing speed, and counting the number of skips each girl could accomplish.

Eevie, Ovie, ca' the rope ower', was the chant in Bute, continuing:

> Mother's in the market
> Selling penny baskets,
> Baby's in the cradle
> Playing wi' the ladle.

In Perthshire it was

> Mother's at the Market
> Wi' her new basket,

and the baby was still in the cradle playing with the ladle. It's that baby again in Fochabers:

> Yanky-panky-sugar-ally-anky,
> Baby's in the cradle
> Playin' wi' the ladle.

Some chants were very brief, as in Argyllshire:

> Blue bell,
> Cockle shell,
> One, two, three,

and Auchmithie's cliff-side skipping went to

> One, two, three, one two, three,
> What a lot o' fisher-wifies I can see!

'The wind blows high', which properly belongs to the marriage ritual, and is found among singing games, has been co-opted for skipping and has come to be regarded as a skipping rhyme.

Skipping rhymes frequently became tagged on to each other, the skippers chanting snippets of rhymes as they occurred to them, for the sake of continuity, and filling the gaps caused by forgetfulness – any rhyme would do so long as the skipping game was not interrupted.

In Glen Gairn, we skipped in the playground with one big rope which two girls ca'd and all the others skipped through in rapid succession 'to keep the pottie boiling', an unwitting corruption of 'to keep the pot a-boiling'. Other games were complex and required much practice to make performance perfect. Variations were devised on the ordinary 'One, two, three, and OUT' routine, such as 'One, two, three a peppery', or 'a hettie' (hottie) when the speed was doubled; or a second girl would go in when the first girl had done only two skips, which meant there were always two under the rope at a time. We might ring the changes by chanting 'One no' miss, two no' miss', up to 'ten no' miss' or more. When you missed you were OUT and had to take a turn at ca'ing the rope. Belgian skipping was when the rope was turned over three times while we jumped once. French Ropes called for skilful manipulation of two ropes, both turning inwards; when the ropes were turned outwards that was known as German Ropes and was even more difficult. In another game, using two ropes, one rope was laid on the ground, kept straight and taut by the girls at each end standing on it while they ca'd the other rope in the usual way. Every girl in the long line had in turn to skip first on one side of the grounded rope, then on the other. If she touched it she was OUT.

'Snakes' is a very old game remembered by many. One player knelt, holding one end of a rope, the other end being loose. The object was to snake the rope along the ground, while the girls attempted to jump over it. The first to touch it was OUT and had to take a turn at snaking the rope.

From Sanquhar came a rhyme that called for appropriate actions. Inspired by the First World War, it commanded:

> Stand at ease,
> Bend your knees,
> Salute the King,
> Bow to the Queen,
> And turn your back to a German.

Edinburgh children, according to Agnes, recited

> I am a Girl Guide dressed all in blue,
> These are the actions that I have to do,
> Bow to the Queen, Salute the King,
> And turn your back on the Kaiser.

Alternative actions for the Girl Guide all dressed in blue are suggested by Ann:

> Stand at ease, bend your knees,
> Bow to the West, salute to the East.

(Then the skipper had to stop the swinging rope by standing on it.) Another rhyme told a fanciful story:

> I am a Girl Guide dressed all in green,
> My mother didn't want me so she sent me to the Queen,
> The Queen didn't want me so she sent me to the King,
> The King said, 'Close your eyes and count to sixteen'.

(After sixteen skips it was the turn of another girl.)

129

Eleanor, an Edinburgh mother, recently heard her children skipping to this chant:

> Marilyn Monroe,
> Went out in the snow,
> Her skirts flew up
> And the boys said 'Oh!'

When she asked them, 'Who was Marilyn Monroe?', they had no idea. Obviously they had never heard that in a film called *The Seven Year Itch* she walked over a ventilator shaft and the hot air lifted her skirt, giving rise to the jingle.

A reminder of a much older rhyme came from Lanark:

> One, two, sky blue, all OUT but you!
> Cups and saucers, plates and dishes,
> See the wee man with the tartan britches!

On the last line each girl had to run out from under the rope, and with both hands, flick up her skirt at the back.

One of the oldest nursery rhymes we learned as children was:

One, two, buckle my shoe, three, four, close the door;
Five, six, pick up sticks, seven, eight, lay them straight;
Nine, ten, a good fat hen, eleven, twelve, see me delve;
Thirteen, fourteen, maids a-courting,
Fifteen, sixteen, maids a-kissing,
Seventeen, eighteen, maids a-waiting;
Nineteen, twenty, my plate's empty.

From Auchterarder came a skipping game with actions, which appears to have its origin in the above nursery rhyme (with overtones of 'Nick, nack, paddy whack, give a dog a bone, This old man came rolling home').

> Number one, touch your thumb,
> Number two, touch your shoe,
> Number three, touch your knee,
> Number four, touch the floor,
> Number five, make a hive,
> Number six, pick up sticks,

Number seven, jump to heaven,
Number eight, jelly on a plate,
Number nine, what's the time?
Number ten, a big fat hen!

In Auchterarder too, skipping and acting out the fictional drama of Lord Nelson at the Battle of Trafalgar, called for special actions:

First, he lost one arm,
Then he lost the other arm;
Next he lost one eye,
Then he lost the other eye.

(By this time the girls were hopping on one leg, arms behind their backs, and both eyes closed.)

And then he dropped down dead.

(Collapse on ground.)

Dumbarton girls called their rope game 'Jumps'. It required three girls at each end to ca' a very heavy rope which stretched from one side of the back-street to the other. The other girls ran in one after the other, jumped, and ran out, chanting, 'Black sugar, White sugar, etc.'

In Strathmiglo and Kirriemuir they did slow jumping from side to side of a swaying rope, while chanting,

Queen Mary, Queen Mary, my age is sixteen,
My faither's a fermer on yonder green,
He has plenty o' siller tae dress me sae braw,
But nae bonnie laddie will tak' me awa',

which was followed by fast skipping to 'Salt, vinegar, mustard, pepper', till they were breathless. They then reverted to slow skipping to a mournful rhythm:

Ding, dong, the castle bell,
So fare thee well, my mother,
Bury me in the old churchyard
Beside my only brother.
My coffin shall be black,
Six white angels at my back,
Two to sing, and two to pray,
And two to carry my soul away.

131

Emily recalls skipping to this obtuse rhyme:

> My wee shoe
> Dressed in blue
> Died last night at half past two,

and remarks, 'Even as a child I thought this a very silly rhyme; only now do I begin to wonder if 'shoe' is perchance a corruption of the French endearment 'chou'.

In Argyll the girls had a rhyme about a little dancing doll . . .

> I had a little doll
> Her name was Cis,
> She did a little dance
> And she stopped like this.

Other rhymes told a story, as in Glasgow's

> I've a laddie in America,
> I've a laddie in Dundee,
> I've a laddie in Australia,
> An' he's comin' back tae mairry me.

> First, he took me tae America,
> Then he took me tae Dundee,
> Then he ran awa' an' left me,
> Wi' three bonnie bairnies on my knee.

> Yin wis sittin' by the fireside,
> Yin wis sittin' on my knee,
> Yin wis sittin' on the doorstep,
> Cryin' 'Daddy, come back tae me!'

A Brechin bairn skipped slowly to

> Raspberry, blackberry, strawberry jam,
> What is the name of my young man?

Then she skipped very quickly through the letters of the alphabet, to discover his initials. To trip on a letter gave his first name – in the same way, the initial of his surname was discovered.

In Aberdeen, while one skipped, the others chanted,

> Black sugar, white sugar, strawberry jam,
> Tell us the name of your young man.

Skipping rapidly through the alphabet was called 'fieries' and 'if you wanted her to trip on a certain letter you just tickled her'. The next question was,

'Will he love you? Yes, No, Yes, No' (*very fast*).
'What will he be? Tinker, Tailor, Soldier, Sailor,
    Rich man, poor man, governor, king' (*slowly*).
'What will you be married in? Silk, satin, muslin, rags'
    (*fast*).
'When? This year, next year, sometime, never' (*fast*).
'Where will you live? Big hoose, little hoose, pig-sty,
    barn' (*slow*).

A girl in Angus skipping with her own rope might chant:

Stockings red, garters blue,
Trimmed all round with silver,
A red, red rose upon my head,
And a gold ring on my finger.
Tell me, tell me, where I was born
Over the hills amang the green corn'

(followed by the alphabet).
In Glen Gairn, rhymes for solo skipping were:

I'll tell Mamma when I get home
The boys won't leave the girls alone,
They pull my hair and break my comb,
And I'll tell Mamma when I get home,

and:

One, two, three, four, five, six, seven,
All good children go to Heaven,
When they die their sin's forgiven,
One, two, three, four, five, six, seven,

or:

Johnnie Raw shot a craw,
Took it hame tae his Ma-maw,
His Ma-maw ate it aw'
An' left the banes for Johnnie Raw,

whereas in Galloway, it was more likely to be:

Brown bread an' brandy-o,
On a summer's mornin'-o,
Gin I had a watch-an'-chain
I'd gie it tae ma Johnnie-o!

In Perthshire they often used these rhymes:

Matthew, Mark, Luke, and John,
Haud the cuddy till I loup on,
Haud it fast, and haud it sure,
Will I win ower the misty muir,

or this version:

Matthew, Mark, Luke, an' John,
Haud the cuddy till I win on,
Haud him siccar an' haud him fair,
Haud him by a pickle hair!

Also from Perthshire:

Penny on the water,
Tuppence on the sea,
Thruppence on the railway,
An' OUT goes she!

and:

I came to a river and I couldn't get across
I paid ten shillings for an old blin' horse,
I jumped on its back, and its bones gave a crack,
An' we a' played the fiddle till the boat came back.

This somewhat morbid rhyme, which was often inscribed on the front page of a new school-book, was sometimes used for skipping:

Johnnie Nory is my name
And Scotland is my nation;
Moniaive's my dwelling-place,
My place of habitation.
When I'm dead and in my grave,
And all my bones are rotten,
This little book will remember me
When I am quite forgotten.

In Ayr they skipped to

> I wish I were a boaby,
> A big, fat boaby,
> Tae wash ma mither's loaby
> Wi' soft soap an' soadie.
> But when the soadie meltit,
> I got ma bottom skelpit.

They followed this by going through the alphabet doing 'fasties', and also some fast skipping to 'Silk, satin, velvet, print, linen, rags'.

Two skipping rhymes from Leith:

> Down to the baker's shop
> Hop, hop, hop!
> For my mother said,
> 'Buy a loaf of bread.'
> Down to the baker's shop
> Hop, hop, hop!

This belongs to the 1930s:

> Up and down, Up and down,
> All the way to London Town.
> Swish, swosh, swish, swosh,
> All the way to King's Cross.
> Legs swung, legs swing,
> All the way to Berlin,
> Head, toe, head, toe,
> All the way to Jericho.

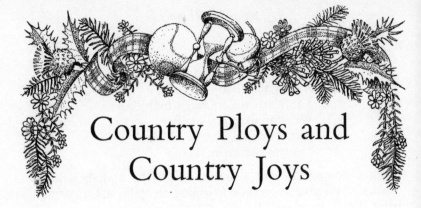

Country Ploys and Country Joys

I, Wullie Wastle, stan' here on ma Castle,
An' a' the dugs in your toon
Canna ding Wullie Wastle doon.

'When I see bairns the day whizzin' doon the road in school-buses, fegs! I whiles feel sorry for them runnin' aboot on wheels instead o' usin' their legs! Fine dae I ken that times has changed, an' that bairns are noo better fed, better cled, better provided for an' get a' thin' laid on that money can buy, but that's jist the point – there's a lot o' things that money canna buy.' So mused Elizabeth in her thoughtful way, and I, listening to her reminiscences, knew what was in her mind.

Mina told me 'There were no expensive toys in our day, nor had we any sense of privation. Children do not really need expensive toys to keep them happy; we made our own. We had great fun with tin cans, smooth stones, and odd bits of wood and string. We lived an out-of-doors life fifty years ago in Midlothian, and the village street was our playground.'

Nigel reminds us that 'all sorts of equipment are now, in many places, provided for children at play. In my boyhood we were thrilled to bits when two sets of swings were erected in our public park. One was labelled BOYS and the other GIRLS, and they were set as far apart as space would permit. They were chained up at night and on Sundays.'

There were special seasons for skipping-ropes and bows and arrows, for catapults and slings, for stilts and jews' harps (derived from jaws' harps) which the loons called their

136

tromps. The hoop, the kite and marbles are among the most ancient of toys and my generation had its own version of them all. Bows and arrows were home-made. A supple sapling made the bow, trimmed and bent, with a piece of fine twine attached to each end. Arrows were short, straight hazel-sticks pointed by the diligent use of a pocket-knife. Slings and catapults were easily contrived from string and bits of leather, forked sticks and indiarubber.

Wind toys like kites and paper windmills were enjoyed everywhere on windy days. Kites were made of newspaper and two birch saplings tied together, balanced by a few twisted screws of paper tied on the long tail. We made a hefty clew of all the pieces of string on which we could lay our hands, took our kite to the high field on a windy day, and amazing to relate, it actually flew!

A springtime ploy in Forfar was the making of a skatie, or draigon, for a kite. They believed that your draigon would not fly unless you shouted as you tossed it skywards,

> A' the birdies in the air
> Tickle on tae my taillie!

At Burghead, old newspapers and basins of flour-paste were required to cover the frame, and herring-nets were used for the tail of the kite. Now, I believe, children can go to the shops and buy a kite for about twenty pence.

Ca'in' a gird was one of our chief delights in summer – not the slow-moving wooden hoop which had to be struck intermittently with a stick, but a lively gird spurred on by a cleek to guide or stop it at will. There was skill in the hand that pursued a clattering gird down winding roads and braes. The local blacksmith made girds for a copper or two, and repaired them without charge when that was necessary.

'I was the daughter of the blacksmith in St Monance', says Ann. 'He made dozens of iron girds. We ran races with them to see who could run fastest and keep our girds going longest. We must have run miles, either for pleasure or when going messages. There was no hardship in running a mile or two to carry a message for no reward but mebbe a jeely piece, as long as we could take our girds.' The sight of a blacksmith working at his craft has attracted bairns since time began. When we

heard the tinka-tinka-tink coming from the small thatched
building near the school, we ran to watch Donal at his anvil,
blinking as our eyes became accustomed to the gloom, for the
interior was lit only by the glow of the furnace. We never
wearied of the clang of the hammer on the anvil, of the great
roar of the huge brass-studded leather bellows with long
handles laboriously pumped by hand, and of watching the
sparks fly to all corners as Donal unerringly brought down the
hammer on the piece of dripping white metal. It was fun, too,
to see the sparks fly when Donal was shoeing a horse, and I
remember the strange smell of burned hooves.

In Springtime, on the swings in the park, and at home in the
garden, the cry would often go up, 'Gie's a shuggie!' When
Perthshire boys took turns in pushing their pals on the swings
they sometimes chanted

> A butcher, a baker, a candlestick maker,
> They all jumped out of a rotten potato,
> With a high shoogie shoo,
> And a low shoogie shoo,
> And a high shoogie shoo to the bargain!

Then they 'let the cat die', which was allowing the swing to
stop.

In the Nor' East the chant was

> See Saw, Margery Daw,
> Tweedle-um, toodle-um, twenty-three,
> A high swee an' a low swee
> An' a swee tae mak the cat dee!

The same rhyme, more or less, did for chanting on a see-saw –
we never had a real one, only a plank resting on a barrel, and
for the littlins we sang over and over 'Showdy, powdy,
showdy, powdy' as we see-sawed them up and down.

In Shetland they also contrived a see-saw:

> We'd finn a aald plank noo an dan
> An hyst him wi' a hunk
> Ipo da nearest staen we fan
> An rig a hedderkin dunk.

An dan for oors we'd rise an faa
Till childish cares wis tint,
Weelno, I widna say just aa,
For we were sair ahint!

'There was often a flurry of snow in April before the last of
the cold weather. It was called the Teuchat Storm, because
teuchats, or pee-wits, were laying their eggs about the time
the snow came', recalls John. 'When I was a boy at school sixty
years ago my pals and I used to collect teuchats' eggs and sell
them. We got ten shillings a dozen, which was a fortune to us
lads before the First World War. The shells were used for
making dye. We collected the eggs in the fields round the
school during the dinner-break, and often were far away when
the bell rang for afternoon school, and if we were late we got
the tawse.'

Birds'-nesting, now looked at askance, was in Victorian
times a manly and socially acceptable pastime for boys. It also
had a disciplinary code. Every boy-collector knew that one
egg only should be taken, and it should be blown at home so
that no trace of its removal should be left on the spot, nor
should the ground and the surrounging growth be disturbed.
It was a matter of pride in a Victorian childhood for a boy to
have a varied collection of eggs, labelled, dated, docketed with
its place of origin, and kept in graded drawers in his very own
egg-cabinet.

'We boys always carried our catapults tucked under our
jerseys in the village of Ford', confesses Lawrie. 'The old
church-bell was a tempting target, high in its steeple, for the
nail-cuttings we acquired in the smiddy as ammunition. If you
did score a ding you had to run for your life before the
superintendent of the Sunday School, who lived nearby, could
catch you. "You could go to hell for that", he often told us
sternly, but we believed that would only be if he caught you at
it, hence the need for speed.'

Digging for worms for bait, then setting off with home-
made rod and line for a day's fishing in the hill-burns like the
Milton, or Daldownie, or the Allt-dubh-iasgan (The burn of
the black trout); or trying to catch podders in the docks, or
newts, frogs, and tadpoles in quarry-holes, are among

boyhood memories. A nature-lover in Castle-Douglas encouraged boys to keep their eyes open and gave a prize to the boy who could bring him the first tadpole.

Lindsay remembers vividly his first real fishing rod. 'When I was twelve, three of us decided to make real fishing-rods, and repaired to the local joiner who would supply the right kind of wood for the purpose and taper the rods for us. We scraped our rods with the edge of a piece of broken glass till we had a really smooth three-piece tapered rod, and then saved up our pennies for the other necessary mountings and reel. We were really proud of them and sallied forth hoping to catch the biggest fish ever seen!'

In connection with fishing, a story has come to light of a wee Angus laddie who agreed, in Sunday School, that Noah in the Ark might possibly have fished in his spare time, but pointed out that 'he couldna get fishin' verra long'. Why? 'Because he'd only got twa wurrums!'

Guddlin' for trout in the nearest burn was something no country bairn could resist.

> Guddlin' in the burn Sandy fand a troot,
> Gruppit it by the gills and smertly flang it oot.
> He didna need a worm, he didna need a flie,
> Bit soopleness o' haun, and glegness in his e'e.
> He built a bonnie fire to roast his caller fish . . .
> It aye tastes better stickit nor servit in a dish.

Children who lived near a burn often used odd pieces of wood as boats. In Shetland they sailed their seggi-boats by taking an iris-leaf, bending the tip over to engage in a crack made farther up, and then sending their boats down the burn to see whose boat would go farthest. 'We boys made out own penny whistles from canes or other hollow stems, like the herd-laddie in Charles Murray's poem, who "cut a sappy sucker frae the muckle rodden tree," and "ye should hae seen the whustle that the wee herd made!" We carved our initials on trees as soon as we acquired a pocket-knife', Ian recalls 'the higher up the tree the better. Alas! Progress has overtaken all the trees and my initials have gone with them!'

'In the village of Doune, where I was born eighty years ago', remarks George, 'there is a large boulder which in the last

140

century was called locally "The Deil's Heid". In my childhood days the village children used to join hands and dance round the boulder singing

> Olie, Olie, peep, peep, peep,
> Here's the man wi' the cloven feet,
> Here's his heid but whaur's his feet?
> Olie, Olie, peep, peep, peep!

I learned from my mother that this was a time-honoured custom in Doune.'

Cathie spent her holidays in Caithness and remembers taking the petals of the large scarlet poppies, turning back the petals and fastening them with grass; then she stuck in parts of the stem to make legs and arms for dollies. 'Like country bairns everywhere, we made necklaces of rose-hips, we pretended to tell the time by blowing away those fluffy heads of dandelion flowers in full seed: "One o'clock, two o'clock, all round the clock", till all the seeds were blown away. When picking the petals off a daisy we repeated the Scots version of "He loves me, He loves me not". As each petal fell we chanted:

> One I love, two I love, three I love, I say,
> Four I love with all my heart, five I throw away;
> Six he loves, seven he loves, eight both love,
> Nine he comes,
> Ten he tarries,
> Eleven he comes,
> Twelve he marries.

'We tested each other with buttercups held under the chin, relieved to see the faint golden reflection that proved we did indeed like butter.'

'We were well-fed but, of course, perpetually hungry', Emma relates, 'and we managed to find all sorts of edible things out-of-doors. The vegetable garden and fruit bushes provided the most obvious source of wealth – peas, beans, carrots, turnips, nasturtiums, currants, berries, and rhubarb dipped in sugar. We pulled the flower-heads from the "dusty millers" and sucked them for their sweetness. Farther afield, we ate the fresh green leaves of the hawthorn – this we called

Seggi-boat

"bread and cheese". The soft white centres of thistles we called "thistle cheese". We ate the tiny pods of the purple vetch and sourocks' shiny green leaves with pointed lobes growing in the lush grass. We picked lamb's tongue plantains, which we called carl doddies, to indulge in mock battles, the object of which was to knock off the heads of our opponents' carl doddies. (Carl originally stood for Charles, otherwise Bonnie Prince Charlie, and Doddy was a corruption of George, the King known as German Geordie.)'

'My memories of village life are very precious to me', says Mina. 'We were poor in material things and did not know it! We played happily, laughed and sang, while our hard-working parents took care of us and somehow managed to provide food and clothing for us all.'

'We went for picnics in the woods' says Jean, 'with lemonade and plenty of sandwiches. We took a large sack with us and filled it with sticks to take home for kindling the fire. We played in the Cuddy's Park in summer and decked each other with daisy and buttercup chains, and how nice we all looked! I was eight years old when we sometimes went to a show in the village hall. The charge for getting in was a jam jar, and many a good show we saw!'

Ena remembers when she was a child in Nithsdale during the First World War, 'we often had a picnic at the burnside where we paddled. My aunt, knitting socks for soldiers, would stop for a little to read a Waverley Novel to my sister and me, as she did on long winter evenings (though once it was *The Count of Monte Cristo* and the last exciting pages were missing!). Aunt Addy, in sealskin jacket or feather boa, smelling of lavender water, walked with us to church on Sunday – there was no public transport. After dinner we wrote letters or went for a walk. Being a strict Sabbatarian, Aunt would not permit us to sew, or to read unsuitable books, or handle toys. We could play no games except 'The Minister's Cat', and 'Word Making and Word Taking', provided the letters spelt a text – but Aunt Addy continued to knit socks for soldiers!'

Ena also recollects that in her childhood the village children went barefoot from May to October, walking sometimes three or four miles along dusty, stony roads to school. In winter they wore brass-bound clogs which she envied because they kept the feet dry and comfortable in cold wet weather. 'Once, I lived in Thornhill, not far from Dumfries', she says, 'a quiet village smelling of limes, which nevertheless produced men of mark, and worthies such as Joseph Thompson, the African explorer, Dr Wallace Williamson, a Moderator of the Church of Scotland, and Dr King Hewitson, a writer on archaeology, with his three austere sisters who wore toques and feather boas. There were several pairs of highly respected sisters, the elder always the more revered. The minister was a tall, frail, saintly-looking man, but thunderous in the pulpit. He lent me many books to read. There was an old shoemaker, John Skillen, a great reader, especially of Scott. I can see him now in his white apron and cloth cap, his game leg, and his family of Dandie Dinmonts in the corner of his but-and-ben. Once, for a treat, a farmer going to Edinburgh took John to visit his birthplace *en route*. On the return journey through Ettrick John asked to get out of the car, and was found kneeling at the grave of the Ettrick Shepherd. Another passenger in the car casually said, "Who was this James Hogg – some Covenantin' body?" There was an awful silence till the passenger was dropped at Morton Mains farm many miles on, when John muttered "Sic ignorance! Sic gross ignorance!", and said not another word. Recently, glancing at a book on dogs, I found a chapter about old John and discovered that he had been one of the foremost authorities on Dandie Dinmonts, and had had a strain called after him.'

'Summer was a great time in Perth', says Lindsay. 'We boys

Aunt Addy

144

went swimming, walking four or five miles to get a swim. At school we played cricket and rounders with home-made bats.'

'In my boyhood in the Border Hill Country there was a lot of wrestling (Cumberland style) among the young lads', muses Malcolm; and James says, 'we went in for wrestling and running in Tarves, running three miles on a summer evening. We thought nothing of cycling ten miles on our five-bob-bikes to play football in Old Meldrum'. Country lads often played football in summer. It was their chief game in Southwick in the years before the First World War.

I remember stopping one day on my way to Southwick School to watch with delight, in a farm pig-sty, eight fat piglets with curly tails, snuggling against the old sow and having a hearty breakfast, and I look back on a holiday in Islay. There, a favourite pig had, unknown to us, been taken away to be killed. Its owner tried to soften the blow for us children faced with an empty sty, by telling us, in her soft Highland voice, 'The lit-tle peeg hass gone to choin its May-ker.'

Muriel describes how, 'In Morayshire, we used to go for picnics to the peat-moss where Father toiled away on the lonely bog. We took hard-boiled eggs from our own hens, sandwiches of roast chicken (one of our own), home-made scones, jam made from wild rasps, and fresh butter in a newly-washed cabbage-leaf. We had no such thing as a fitted picnic-case, and no thermos flask. We had cold tea, and milk warm from the cow, all packed in an ordinary basket covered with a towel bleached white in the sun. It was so peaceful sitting on that moor . . . nothing to be seen but miles and miles of heather, wild flowers, and an occasional rowan-tree on guard to keep evil spirits away from some lonely larach.'

'Picnics were summer glories in Nithsdale', Ena re-members. 'We walked four and a half miles to the hills, or to Morton Castle, carrying, not thermos flasks and dainty sandwiches, but baskets filled with new-baked scones, fresh butter and home-made jam, and substantial sandwiches packed in fancy napkins. We carried a kettle, a large pewter tea-pot complete with cosy. The sun beat on our backs as we staggered up the brae, but we knew the load would be lighter when we returned. On arrival, two went to the farm for milk, two to gather sticks for the fire, and others to get water from

Sunday and Aunt Addy

146

the burn. We lit a fire and while we waited for the kettle to boil, we spread the cloth, placing stones at the four corners, and set out the feast – sandwiches, soda, treacle, and tattie scones, and pancakes. Afterwards the boys went to fish up the cleuch, and we girls played around and did a little climbing on the gentle slopes of the hills, and swiped in futile fashion at the midges who came to feast on *us*; there was no defence against them; they thrived on smoke, and parried all our attempts at swatting them! Then came the long trek home, tired but happy, with fish the boys had caught and possibly mushrooms or wild rasps that we had gathered. I remember once, after a promising evening, preparations were made for a picnic and the next day was wet, so, instead, we had a very happy picnic on the stairs and on the broad landing.'

At haymaking time in Glen Gairn we loved to jump over the coles which, like upturned Christmas puddings, dotted the fields. In autumn, we gathered hazel-nuts, cracking them on a stone and eating the kernels on the spot. We also went out with baskets to gather blaeberries and brambles, wild grossets, and brawlins, and those who lived near the higher hills brought home cranberries and averins; all these were made into jams to stock the family store cupboard.

In Shetland the game of skoili-moili, a form of hide-and-seek, was played on moonlight nights at harvest-time when the corn was in stook. Later, played among the cornstacks by moonlight, it was called by the older folk 'skoit-a-mill-a-skroo'. In Orkney, Walter tells us, the same game was played among the stooks, and there they called it playing dinkie doos among the skroos.

'We used to dig up little bulbs or nuts that grew in the ground beneath a special type of couch grass', Malcolm recalls. 'They tasted like hazel-nuts, and were known as tiger-nuts; we used to make weird noises by blowing through a broad blade of grass held edgewise between our thumbs. We also chewed sourocks which tasted rather like bitter lemon, and raw nettle leaves which we rubbed in our fingers before eating them. As we did not get stung we liked to show off this trick.'

'Living on the outskirts of Edinburgh as we did', writes Jem, 'when our buttercup field was built over, we played on the partially-built houses, balancing on the foundation beams. When my lightweight cousin leaned against a chimney-piece the fireplace collapsed, leaving us with a sense of guilt and a permanent bias against modern housing! We reverted after that incident to our former historical games, embracing Bonnie Prince Charlie and the Marquis of Montrose.'

Boys still sally forth in autumn as they have done for generations to gather conkers from horse-chestnut trees. The varnished mahogany-looking conker is the prize and preoccupation of every boy. Sometimes they hold them in front of the fire to harden them. They bore a hole in a conker, pass a strong string through, with a good knot on the end by which the conker is held. Every boy has a shottie at trying to knock out his opponents' conkers. The rules can be simple or complex, and a strict note is kept of the number of smash hits. In some places conkers are called chessies. In Glasgow they were called 'Bully Nuts'.

'In Winter, tobogganing, snowballing, skating and sliding on ice, and making snowmen were the order of the day. This was the time for games with a lot of running about to keep you warm. We could usually count on a few days skating from about November,' Lindsay remembers, 'Our skates were wooden, with a screw into the heel of the boot and a strap over the toe, and a single blade.' Jim used to go sliding downhill on a large piece of cardboard or tin, 'or if we were lucky, a large tin-tray, better still, one of the old-fashioned metal-tiled plates which fitted across the hearth. It was healthy entertainment and braw fun!'

It may have been an old Scots laird who first called to invaders of his stronghold

> *I* am the King of *this* Castle
> Get down, you dirty rascal!'

Ever since, any hillock or slight eminence has served for little loons to mount, as they used to do in Berwick, and shout defiance to their attackers:

> I, Wullie Wastle, stan' here on ma castle,
> An' a' the dugs in *your* toon
> Will no' drive Wullie Wastle doon!

148

'In Olaberry, in Shetland, children used to scramble over the walls of deserted buildings, to defend the ruins of *their* castle from invading "Roman soldiers". My memories of a childhood in Ronasvoe', says Marguerite, 'include playing Blind Man's Buff, which in Shetland is called "Bawkie Blin', the Blin' Bogie", and the sheer enjoyment of Heddercandunk, and the fun we had when we were sent to the hills to gather in the sheep. We picked handfuls of cotton sedge, which we called 'Lukkie's 'oo.'

Flora describes rooin' the sheep when the finest wool was plucked by hand, and the rest was sheared with very small shears. She recalls how all the children wore ribblins (or rivlins) which were sandals fashioned by hand from cowhide. Little girls used to gather hentins, or hintie leggits, the tufts of wool they found adhering to the drystane dykes on the hills, and with them lined shoe-boxes to make cosy beds for their dolls.

'Before the First World War', Ena remembers, 'there was a little yellow ambulance attached to the hospital in Nithsdale. One horse was used for a local emergency, two for a distant case. The horses were hired from the man who ran the bus to the station a mile away, meeting each train. In winter the "bus" was an old cab with candle-lamps; the cabbie wore a varnished bowler-hat. In summer when the visitors (not yet labelled tourists) arrived, there was a char-à-banc. When excursions were arranged, *young* passengers would be requested to get down and walk up the hills to spare the horses. This had the expected effect of emptying the chara! I recall being sent to the Stables to order a horse and open carriage to go for a country drive. As the War continued, horses were called up, and the Stables and local doctor acquired motor-cars.'

Fun at the Seaside

When we were Co'en' laddies up tae mony a bairnies'
    pranks
Fu' mony a happy 'oor we spent at bonnie Sou'dick
    Bank,
We jinkit roon the Needle's Ee an' nettit shrimps an'
    prawns,
But aye we hurriet hame for tea an' ane o' Auntie's
    scones.

As ilka ane reached manhood's prime we left thae scenes
    endearin',
But aye gaed back in simmer-time tae try the flounder-
    spearin',
An' when the tide cam ower the sand, oor leisterin' sport
    wis gone,
We'd clamour, as we hameward ran, for a newly-bakit
    scone.

All down the years children have loved to play on the
sea-shore, sometimes with wooden spades, like Robert Louis
Stevenson as a child, digging holes in the sand for the tide to
fill up and calling them sea-wells. 'We loved to play with
water', writes Louisa, 'a natural delight often denied children
today. All we needed to keep us happy was a tin can, a piece of
red brick and water. We rubbed the brick on the edge of a
rock-pool till the water was coloured red . . . we called it
"making red milk". We scooped it into cans and emptied it
into other pools. It kept us amused for hours, forgetful of

everything but the making of red milk. The incoming tide washed away our efforts but, on returning when the tide went out we still had our favourite rocks with their own little pools waiting for us to start all over again. My grandfather was the well-known boat-builder at Gourdon; The Slough, a wide passage through the rocks to the deep water where the boats were launched still bears his name, Jeems' Slough. Not every fishing village has an area of grass-land adjacent to the sea, but Gourdon had. Sea greens was the name given to it. Fierce high tides in winter caused erosion, tearing apart large clumps which looked like islands. We called them Our Islands and when the tide came in we jumped from island to island for hours on end, thoughts of home only flashed upon us when we fell in and got wet!

'There were some very dangerous places among the rocks where we were forbidden to go. We were told the kelpies would get us if we disobeyed. This we believed and were afraid to be disobedient. Occasionally we saw live seals which the fishermen brought in; these we thought were kelpies, and when we sighted a school of porpoises we thought they were kelpies waiting to take us away if we were naughty.'

According to Shetland lore the seals have a King and the crows a Court of Justice. Shetland children learn that according to tradition,

> The crows' court metes out justice stern
> At times in the secluded hills,
> And on lone skerries by the shore
> The Seal King rules his soft-eyed kind
> And guards them by his secret lore
> Against the malice of mankind.

At Olaberry, children used to catch crabs, set them in a row, and watch them 'running races'.

Elizabeth describes how 'In Leven, during the school holidays, we used to take a bottle of drinking-water and a jeely piece to the park. Every village and town had its Park. Sometimes we went to the shore and collected whelks which we called buckies. There was a saying, "Awa' tae Banff an' gaither buckies". We built a fire and boiled them in an old tin can. We boiled them three times (we called it three froths) then they were ready to eat.'

'Catching bandies was one of our ploys', says James. 'These were minnows. We kept them in jam-jars and looked after them. We also collected frog-spawn, our object being to see which of us could keep the spawn and the tadpoles till frogs developed! With a rod made from a garden-cane, black linen thread from the sewing-machine drawer, and hooks retrieved from those discarded by fishermen before they reached the waste-bin, we fished for podlies, using as bait mussels which we found among the rocks.'

Effie recalls that a splendid ploy at the seaside was to find all sorts of coloured bits of stone, to grind them into little heaps of powder when marvellous shoppies could then be stocked with tea, sugar, coffee, lentils, etc. An orange provided quite a lot of goods for a shoppie. The pips were eggs, and the peel was rolled up and tied with thread to become bacon. The orange itself was usually eaten by the shop-keeper!

'Only in the summer holidays had we time to play housies', says Mary. 'We chose a rocky background with little ledges to do duty as dressers and mantel-pieces. For ornaments we selected bits of jetsam, and shells for dishes. We made walls for our housies with stones set in rows on the sand in front of our rocks. Bits of glass and earthenware worn smooth by the action of the tide represented all kinds of things for our housies or shoppies. To make ourselves look older we sometimes made a pair of glasses by hammering the centres out of limpet shells, two of which were then fixed up with a bridge, and "legs" were made with wool or string. We used our old school exercise-books to make paper-boats which we raced. It was amazing how far out to sea they would go.'

'We were very fond of eating seaweed', Louisa remembers, 'especially sea-tangle and dulse, straight off the rocks with a dip in sea-water to remove salt and sand. Crappit Heids was a favourite dish at home. Large cod-heads were boiled till the fish left the bones, which were then removed. The fish was put back in the pan, brought to the boil and seasoned. That was good enough for everyday; for special occasions the cod's heads were stuffed with cod-roe or crab-meat, beaten eggs and breadcrumbs, and the fish-stock was poured over them. I

Pulling the lifeboat

remember how, long ago, the lifeboat on its special carriage with big wheels, was pulled by a long rope from its shed to the harbour. We bairns loved to help to pull it. Groats, or groaties, were our treasures. These tiny shells are only found in certain places. We knew where to find them and used them to make pretty necklaces, and to decorate little boxes and photo-frames as gifts for friends. From time to time we wound a hank of wool very tightly to make a ball, the tighter the better. They were not much use for stotting, and we sometimes placed a piece of cork inside in the hope of getting a better bounce. It had to be done skilfully, otherwise the stotting would be erratic. We got the cork from old cork-floats discarded on the beach.' '

'In Victorian days', relates Flora, 'one of my aunts married a Londoner. She, wishing to show him the charms of Scotland, arranged that on their first holiday, they came to Stonehaven. One morning her husband decided to go for a swim. On his return he remarked that he was surprised to find that the hardy Scots had laid hard little mats on the very stony beach, on which he gladly stepped, trouble-free, into the sea. The "hard little mats", as he called them, were, in reality, good-sized boned cod-fish, without heads or tails, which had been spread out on the stones to dry in the wind and sun! I think that method of drying fish used to be called rizzared or blawn.'

Here is an old song of the fisher-folk of Fife which was familiar to all bairns in the villages along the Fife coast:

> Up wi' the carls o' Dysart
> An' the lads o' Buckhaven,
> An' the kimmers o' Largo,
> An' the lasses o' Leven!
> *Chorus*: Hey ca' thro', ca' thro',
> For we hae meikle ado,
> Hey ca' thro', ca' thro',
> For we hae meikle ado!
>
> We hae tales tae tell
> An' we hae sangs tae sing,
> We hae pennies tae spend,
> An' we hae pints tae bring.
> *Chorus*: Hey ca' thro', etc.
>
> We'll live a' oor days,
> An' them that comes ahin'
> Let them dae the like
> An' spend the gear they win.
> *Chorus*: Hey ca' thro', etc.

Stap is a delicious dish which Shetland children love. It is made with the liver and soft bits of the head of a fish:

> Let idder laans ower Shetland craa
> She doesna care a rap,
> Wi' a rare dish she dings dem aa
> Fresh liver-heads an stap.
>
> O weel I min' a child I sat
> Upon mi midder's lap,
> An' weel I min' I yowled an' grat
> An' skirled oot for stap.

Superstitions

Ring–a–ring a pinkie,
Ring–a–ring a bell;
If I break the bargain
I'll gae tae hell.

Children are natural believers in signs and wonders; they readily take over any old superstition that takes their fancy, and not only make it their own but improve on it, and devise a few to suit themselves. They have been doing it for generations and are still at it today. Here are a few well-known ones that have been recalled, and some that may be new to a few readers.

'My mother, a Lowland Scot, was very superstitious', says Anne, 'and she had one superstition I have never heard from anybody else. When my sister and I had any important exam, Mother would burn the poker in the fire keeping it there during the actual exam hours. We had the shortest poker in the street! She would never cut our finger-nails on Sunday lest they turn into pigs' trotters!'

Forfar bairns learned a rhyme regarding suitable days for the trimming of finger-nails. Early in the week was advisable, for it was

Monday for health,
Tuesday for wealth,
Wednesday for the best day of a'.

155

Later in the week was not propitious because it was

> Thursday for losses,
> Friday for crosses,
> And Saturday no' day at a'.

As a child *I* was told that Friday was an unlucky day for trimming finger-nails. I remember seeing my three little cousins in Stirling over seventy years ago lined up in their Sunday hats, ready for church, and my uncle would then trim their finger-nails. He was not superstitious, but he was a busy man and had no time to trim their nails on any other day.

Country children absorbed superstitions which are now dignified as folk-lore. They believed in 'fairy rings', in 'lucky fits' and 'unlucky fits'. It seems they believed that you were born either lucky or unlucky and there was nothing you could do about it, except take certain precautions, when that was possible.

Buckie bairns chanted

> If you wish to live and thrive
> Let a spider run alive.

(For if you kill it, it brings rain.) Likewise, 'Never stand on a beetle (a "cloaker"), or there will be rain.'

A plea for a favourable weather forecast was

> Snail, snail, shoot oot yer horn
> An' tell me gin it'll be a fine day the morn.

When a bairn fell into a bed of nettles she had to crawl round searching for a docken leaf, with its moisture at the base of the stalk, singing (or more probably whimpering),

> Nettle, nettle gang awa'
> Docken, docken come!

Until she found a dock-leaf with its magical healing properties, she applied her own spittle to the nettle-stings which frequently proved as soothing.

Children still carry on the superstitions which they have picked up from older people, such as that tripping on a step when going upstairs means that there is a marriage in the offing, and that to hear a dog howling at night foretells a funeral.

An itchy nose [say country bairns] is a sign the lads are
   gaunna tease ye,
An itchy palm, that siller's comin' tae ye.

And when they see magpies, they still chant,

>Ane's for joy, but twa's grief,
>Three's a weddin', but fower's deith,
>Five's for a coffin, six for a hearse,
>Seeven's a mannie in great distress.

And this superstition about ponies still appeals to them:

>One white foot, keep him till the end,
>Two white feet, give him to a friend,
>Three white feet, send him far away,
>Four white feet, keep him not a day.

  At a school in Edinburgh, when two girls made a
simultaneous exclamation, they at once, without saying
another word, linked their pinkies, Ring-a-ring-apinkie style,
and waited till someone came along and, with a chopping
movement, broke the spell.

  Another occasion for silence was when going under a
bridge. Walking under a ladder had to be avoided but all
would be well if you made a secret wish, or kept your fingers
crossed. You must always give a coin in exchange for a present
of scissors, a pocket-knife, or anything else that had a sharp
point, in case you 'cut' the friendship or goodwill.

  It was unlucky to wear a new coat unless you first put a coin
or something in the pockets, as was done on Handsel Monday.
At school we pinched the arm of anyone seen to be wearing a
new coat or dress for the first time. This was supposed to bring
them luck. We also gave them 'a pinch and a punch for the first
of the month' running round pinching and punching our best
pals, again for luck; but Emma reminds us that 'if any of our
chums had a new frock or coat, they got "A nip for your new
frock", and a gey sair nip it often was!'

  There was a superstition, too, regarding the straw boaters
men used to wear in summer, straw 'bashers' they were called,
and the custom was, the first straw basher a child saw each
summer, he or she would shout 'Chapsie me!' and spit!

Town bairns, of course, had their own superstitions regarding all those cracks in the pavement. 'If you walk on the cracks it's like breaking your mother's best dishes', said a Perthshire child, but in Kirkcudbright it was 'the Devil's dishes'.

> If ye stan' on a line, ye'll brak yer spine,
> If ye stan' on a crack ye'll brak yer back,

they said in Strathdon, and in Fraserburgh they warned the unwary littlin, 'Dinna walk on the lines or ye'll meet the Deil.' Town bairns used to think it brought good luck for the day if you saw a white horse, a black cat, or a chimney-sweep.

'We had some odd little customs at boarding-school', says Agnes. 'We said "Rabbits" three times the last thing at night on the last day of each month, and "Hares" three times before any other word was uttered in the morning. It was an incantation to bring us good luck for the whole month and was taken seriously. We were quite distressed if we forgot to say it until the day was well-advanced, for that put an end to any hope of getting a present during the month, or even to having a wish granted.

'We said

> See a pin and pick it up, all the day you'll have Good Luck,
> See a pin and let it lie, you'll have Bad Luck ere you die.

In those days there always seemed to be lots of pins to pick up.

'To break a hand-mirror from our dressing-table was a terrible disaster as that meant seven whole years of bad luck.'

The Saturday Penny

Ally bally ally bally bee,
Sittin' on yer mammy's knee,
Greetin' for anither bawbee
Tae buy mair Coulter's Candy.
Little Annie's greetin' tae,
Sae whit can puir wee Mammy dae
But gie them a penny atween them twae
Tae buy mair Coulter's Candy.

Robert Coltart, the 'Coulter' of the song, made his celebrated candy, flavoured with aniseed, in Melrose and sold it there and in Galashiels. He travelled round all the country fairs and markets in the Borders. Children used to troop after him as if he was a Scots Pied Piper. He died in 1890, and is still remembered.

'In the days when it was safe, in more ways than one, to send a bairn for the messages', Mary reminisces, 'I was often sent on a Saturday for syrup or treacle. The grocer placed a jar under a tap connected to a large cask, and I would gaze fascinated as the black or golden liquid slowly made its way into the jar. Treacle was a penny a pound then, and syrup three ha'pence. I got a penny to spend on Saturdays and I used to walk down to the sweetie shop trying to decide how to spend it. Would it be a ha'penny-worth of coconut chips or a pennyworth "all round the shop", taking a bit of toffee off every tray? There were no wrapped sweets then.'

159

Treacle barrel

160

Originally, most of the sweeties that Scots children enjoyed were made simply in a pan over an open fire.

'Seventy years ago in Perth', Lindsay recalls, 'a ha'penny meant something, and was only given if we had dutifully carried out all our chores for the week. With a ha'penny in hand we trotted along to Auld Grannie MacAllister's shoppie, which was the front room in her but–an'–ben, and there we feasted our eyes on rows of bottled "boilings". These were boiled sweets of every kind; there were also trays of syrup and treacle toffee, and "cheuch jeans", a long-lasting candy, so tough it could only be sucked. Auld Grannie on a summer day would sit outside her door, with her mutch and clay pipe, and we had to await her pleasure. A liquorice strap, or "Lether-me-hame", so called because it resembled a leather strap, was a favourite, and could be torn into two long strips. Sometimes Grannie would allow us to take one half in the morning, and collect the other strip in the afternoon. Liquorice nail-rod was another good buy. Like cheuch jeans it was hard to bite, and many a wobbly milk-tooth was lost in this way.'

'This wasn't exactly a game, but, in a way, a commercial enterprise', chuckles George. 'In a field outside our town there was a large stone, or outcrop of rock, known as the Granny's Stone. It was a pleasant spot for a rest on a longish walk. In this stone were several cracks and crevices, and into these we would invite strangers and unwary friends to insert coins "for luck". When the coast was clear, we applied our method of extracting the coins with a pen-knife or a piece of wire. A visit to the nearest sweet-shop followed. The harvest was not great by modern standards, but when it is recalled what could be bought with even the humble ha'penny, the game was not unprofitable. Aniseed balls were considered the best bargain. In those days we called a penny a "wing" and a ha'penny a "maik".'

'When I came up to Glasgow from the country in 1912', Iain recollects, 'there was a back-street dairy that sold home-made pale brown sticky stuff known, for some strange reason, as Ham-an'-Egg Toffee. It was very popular. I have heard my mother speak fondly of spending her Saturday Farthing on "Black Man", which she described as "an old-fashioned, soul-satisfying, delectable sweetmeat". It appears in *The Scots*

Kitchen and was made with treacle, vinegar, and baking-soda. It looked like gingerbread till it was broken up and actually was a crispy chew.'

Buying sweets on Sunday was forbidden and had to be done secretly. An old woman in a shoppie up a close in Castle Douglas sold sweeties on Sunday, and a good few ha'pennies intended for the Sunday School 'collection' went into her till.

'Saturday was a good day for us in Fife', Jean remembers. 'We each got a farthing to spend, and what a picking and choosing there was before we could get what we wanted! A Lucky Potato always had a charm or something inside. You had to suck all the brown off the potato, and the toffee underneath was hard, but you crunched away to get to the centre and the charm wrapped in paper.

'Other sweets were black balls, jelly babies, coconut bars, butter nuts (my favourite) and, in a tray, hard toffee which was cracked with a toffee-hammer before your very eyes.

'We had a chip-cart that came on Saturday. The man's name was Will Cook! He made very good chips and gave us a real bargain for our penny.'

Rob has never forgotten the sweets he bought on a Saturday. 'They were mainly "Throw outs" which a local shop stocked. They were sweets which had been spoiled in the making, and we got a generous portion for our ha'penny.'

In Glasgow, children used to go to the 'Tally Annie's', the Italian ice-cream parlour, in cold weather, to have a basinful of bree, the thickened water in which the peas had been boiled, seasoned with pepper and vinegar. Grown Ups could afford threepence for a plate of peas, and children were happy to have a pennyworth of the bree, and what a shout of glee went up if they found a whole pea! In the early 1900s a portion of fish-an'-chips cost tuppence. The fish-and-chip shops were known as 'chippies'.

'My Mother used to talk of her childhood in Stirling', says Agnes, 'and of the ice-cream seller with his little hand-cart and his perpetual cry of "Hokey Pokey, a penny a lump". He wore a bowler hat and a white apron round his middle, and worked in his shirt-sleeves, diving down to the depths of his cart to extract lumps of his home-made wares. On entering a street he would bang his barrow-lid for attention, and children would follow him, shouting with glee:

> Hokey Pokey, Penny a Lump,
> That's the stuff tae gar ye jump,
> When ye jump ye're sure tae fa',
> Hokey Pokey, that's a'.

'Ice cream in those early days was delicious – thick, custardy, and flavoured with vanilla.'

Margaret remembers that 'from the "Stop me and Buy One" man, pedalling along on his tricycle, we got ha'penny cones, tuppenny wafers enclosing a solid buttery chunk, and thruppenny sponges. A special treat was to have a squirt of raspberry syrup over a wafer which cost thruppence or more. We got huge cornets and thick wafers for a very modest sum.'

Emily says 'Our Saturday Penny was very precious because we seldom received any other money. We spent it on Dolly Mixtures, white-dusted bon-bons and Ogo Pogo Eyes. This was in Airdrie. We also bought cinnamon sticks to nibble or to smoke. We got these from the chemist and the boys used to go into a quiet corner, set the end alight, and smoke them like cigarettes. We bought liquorice stick which was twig-like and yellow. This, we chewed at intervals till it was a soft pale yellow woolly mass.'

Laddies in St Andrews earned their Saturday 'pooch penny' by delivering boots and shoes for the local soutar for the meagre sum of one shilling. They also went caddying for golfers. Tips ranged from the odd copper to a brandy-ball or a pan-drop. The large pan-drops, nearly two inches across, were long-lasting, and when they grew tired of licking one down to size to put in the mouth, they usually put it in their pooch among all the things a normal laddie carried around. It had to be washed now and then! Pomfret cakes were the size of a penny and about as thick. They dissolved far too quickly! Puff Candy in the shape of a heart made from white of egg and sugar, a real Fife speciality, could also be had.

'Going for a message, maybe a mile away, would earn for a bairn a jeely piece, a bun, or perhaps a penny with which you could buy Cowboy Chew, Broken Chocolate, or Toffee Noddles, but best of all was Buttermilk Toffee.

'In those bygone days', says Jim, 'we were lucky to get a prized Saturday Penny. This got you in to the cinema matinée. If I got a ha'penny to spend I bought "spulters" which was damaged fruit. For a ha'penny I would get three apples and three pears and could treat my pals.'

At Country Fairs the toffee seller was always in evidence, with his toffee on a tray supported by a cord round his neck, or laid out on trestle-tables. He also sold it in the streets, shouting, 'Cinnamon Rock! Gether, bairns, gether!'

The reflections of an exiled Scot include 'our sweets in the country in those distant days were the wild fruits that grew all along that northern valley, with the occasional treat of a ha'penny bar of toffee, or a quarter of a pound of cough lozenges from the grocer's van. Ha'pennies were hard to come by. We boys turned them over and over in our pockets while pondering how best to spend them, till they were moist and warm. I recall that on one occasion the grocer looked at me with a twinkle in his eye, and said, as I handed over my treasured coin, "Weel, weel, laddie, ye've had that ane a gey lang time! It's burnin' het!"'

'As children', Alison explains, 'we had little in the way of material possessions, and no regular pocket-money, brandy balls or strippit balls being the most we could aspire to, but we had plenty of other delights, such as tiger nuts from the fields, locust beans, sourocks, or a fine juicy neep bashed against the dyke and eaten in chunks, just like the coos!'

'In Brechin', comments Emma, 'there was toffee we called "Jaw Puller" because you had to pull it out in your jaw till it [the toffee] broke. It almost earned the more realistic name of "Jaw Breaker". There were also large Imperials that changed colour many times, and had to be continually popped out and in of your mouth so that you could observe the colours changing. Sherbet was a favourite of us girls. It was enclosed in a small triangular bag, with a liquorice tube protruding, through which you could suck or dab the effervescent powder. It could also be bought in oval wooden boxes, and a tiny spoon was supplied with which to scoop out the powder, which we called "Kiltie".'

There used to be little pink fondant creams shaped in a cone with a hazelnut on top – one of the delights of a country childhood in Cummertrees. There was also in Edinburgh crystallised sugar candy with string throughout it, bought from the chemist, and Yule Logs which were toffee coated with chocolate and decorated with coconut to resemble snow. These were four a penny and were Alena's favourite sweets, but Catherine preferred 'owl's eyes of many colours because you got sixteen for a penny'.

Chocolate animals with cream inside cost a penny or a ha'penny each, and it was possible to buy a ha'pennyworth of Sweetie Biscuits which were tiny round biscuits with letters of the alphabet in pink and white icing. Ring Rock was a stick of lemon- or vanilla-flavoured rock, about four inches long, with a diamond, ruby or emerald ring on it.

In Aberlour, before the First World War, one could buy a ha'penny cake of 'Trecola', which was treacle toffee, or a ha'penny strip of Rocket Toffee. There was also a thick slice of soft toffee embedded with hazel-nuts and an edging of white sugar icing, which was a penny a slice and very good to eat. Nougat was popular, and twisty starry rock with brown and white stripes. Starry Rock is a traditional Angus sweet which is still made in Brechin, in sticks of various colours and flavours.

'My mouth waters when I recall chocolate beans, tiny coloured jujubes, chocolate truffles and 'oddfellows', which were special lozenges which have been made for over a century by a firm in Wishaw', says Caroline. '"Sugar babies" were for girls – boys thought them cissy!'

'"Ogo Pogo Eyes" were favourite sweets of Gallowgate bairns', as Maureen reminds us. 'They changed colour as they were being sucked. The Ogo Pogo was a legendary monster, said to terrify children with his fearsome eyes.'

All kinds of local delicacies have been mentioned in readers' letters, specialities of the town which gave them their name: for example, Aberdeen Candy, a light brown toffee, had a slight flavour of cloves: Jethart snails still made in Jedburgh, are rounded pieces of toffee with a knot in the centre to represent a small snail. The recipe is said to have come originally from a French prisoner-of-war in Napoleonic times. 'Soor plooms' from Galashiels are pale green, refreshing sweets, slightly acid in flavour. They commemorate the day when English marauders eating unripe plums were surprised and routed by the Braw Lads o' Gala Water. Moffat Whirlies are hard brown toffees twisted with amber, very shiny; Helensburgh Toffee is like fudge, Berwick Cockles are oval sweets with pink stripes and peppermint flavour, Carluke Balls are hard oval sweets, something like peppermint humbugs; Hawick Balls and Torry Pebbles are also hard, but Edinburgh Rock, its fluted sticks of pastel shades and delicate flavours is deliciously creamy and melts in the mouth. It was originally made by the famous firm of Ferguson, and, packed in tartan boxes, went all round the globe. I remember Forfar Rock, too, and the laddie who, wearing a uniform cap too big for his head, carried a tray slung by a broad strap round his shoulder along the station platform, calling out 'Forfar Rock! Forfar Rock!' It may have been the same boy who announced, for good measure, 'famed all over the world'! and a farm lad, to rile him, leaned out of a carriage window and shouted, '*A 've* niver ha'ard o't afore'. The boy took one look at him and retorted, 'It's easy seen *ye* hinna been far!'

James can remember when 'you got eight strippit black balls for a ha'penny' (the kind that used to be taken to church by our grandparents; they calculated that they could suck three in a forty-minute sermon). Striped rock in various colours, and yellow spiral sticks of barley sugar were always great favourites, as was tablet of different flavours. Eight caramels for a ha'penny were chewy and long-lasting. All the sweets were sold by numbers, I never saw anything weighed. Pogo balls were a bigger version of cinnamon balls and changed colour as you sucked. One wee chap, who could not yet speak properly, always spent *his* Saturday penny on "tar-mels" (caramels).'

My father always brought us Easter Eggs of decorated sugar, chocolate eggs came a good while later, chocolate mice, sugar pigs with curly tails, barley sugar, and Callard and Bowser's butter-scotch, a wholesome sweet approved by our parents. We were sometimes given chocolate creams and chocolate drops. Plain drops cost threepence a quarter, and those coated with minute coloured balls, like 'hundreds and thousands', were dearer.

Tuppence was the price of Fry's Chocolate Cream Bars in

Forfar Rock

167

four sections. It is many years since I last saw their advertisement showing the expressive face of a boy in a sailor suit eating chocolate in stages which began with Anticipation and ended in blissful Realisation.

There was, too, a penny cake of plain chocolate, marked in four sections, two of which showed a cocoa bean and the other two a Fry's shield.

We were encouraged to buy fruit instead of sweets which my Mother declared were 'bad for our teeth', though there were, in fact, a wonderful selection which could be obtained for a penny – mint balls, sticks of rock, or a wee bag of Scotch Mixtures, which consisted of small hard white sweets, some round, some oval; the 'curly murlies' had a clove or a carvie imbedded in each, 'curly doddies' were roughened outside, and there was in the mixture a few pink discs of sugar and an occasional sugar almond.

'Cupid's Whispers' were smooth scented rounds of sugar in pastel colours, inscribed in coloured lettering, 'I love you', 'You are my sweetheart', and similar sentiments. Conversation lozenges, or Reading Sweeties, as they were sometimes called, were of different shapes, bright colours and distinctive flavours. Their object was the same as the 'Whispers', to provide a bashful swain with an excuse for approaching his beloved. No party or 'soree' was complete without them.

Elizabeth chimes in with, 'Grandma made the most delicious sweets . . . dates with the stone removed and marzipan inserted, and marzipan potatoes. Of course these sweets were Very Special, not for everyday occasions – oh no!'

Mary describes how your Saturday penny could be eked out by buying two ha'pennyworths on separate occasions and your purchase might well be wrapped in a page from a used school-notebook neatly twisted into a cone. 'By presenting your old exercise-book for this purpose', she explains, 'you could obtain a few free sweets.' A popular fancy was a slab of Trecola costing a ha'penny; there were also bull's eyes, eight for a penny, and almond rock, sold in slabs which were attacked by a special hammer and presented in broken pieces. There were treacle dabs, and liquorice allsorts, the kind with tiny coloured balls of sugar on them; there was Gibraltar rock flavoured with ginger, and Curly Andrews, a sort of comfit, like small pink pan-drops which contained a coriander seed, and sometimes were found in Scotch Mixtures.

'In St Monance', reflects Harriet, 'our main sweets were Rock Bools, real gob-stoppers nearly as big as a golf-ball. We got two for a ha'penny. We also had "Hanky Panky", the name we gave to candy, striped pink and white or yellow and white.'

'In Dreghorn', William remembers, 'ninety years ago, we had several kinds of liquorice sweetmeats, including "Honey Dew", which were pieces ten inches long and half an inch thick. We used to sing, to the tune of "John Brown's Body",

> John Brown's cuddy has a sugar-ally tail
> And it sooks it a' the day!'

This was a reference to Sugar Ally Water which was supposed to be good for coughs and tummy pains. 'We made it' continues Walter, 'by cutting chips off a hard liquorice stick and shaking them up in water till it was brown and fluffy and altogether delicious in our eyes. We kept the bottle under the bed for a time till we considered it was just right for drinking.'

Girls in Perth made Sugar Ally Water and chanted

> Sugar Ally Water, black as the lum,
> Gather up preens an' ye'll a' get some.

Preens were prized, being useful to both boys and girls. The girls allowed one swig for a plain preen, two swigs for a china-headed preen. Passing the bottle round was not very hygienic, but they survived!

Mabel, a Brechin lass, charged a match instead of a preen, and took the matches home to her mother. She, too, kept her Sugar Ally Water in the dark to preserve its colour.

There was a nonsense rhyme which said

> Send for the doctor,
> Out goes the cat,
> In comes a wee man
> Wi' a sugar-ally hat.

Robert remembers that in Edinburgh it was called Sugar Olly. 'Whenever we were lucky enough to get a stick of thick black hard liquorice we would get Mother to break it up for us with the kitchen knife and rolling pin, like breaking Blackpool rock. We put the small pieces in a lemonade bottle filled with cold water and stored it in a dark cupboard for two or three weeks, shaking it vigorously at intervals until the liquorice chips had all dissolved. The resulting liquid was black and had a nice flavour. We used to chant

> Sugar Olly Water, black as the lum,
> Come with your tinnies and you'll all get some.'

Other variations on the Sugar Ally theme were, according to Charlotte, 'Gie's a preen an' I'll gie ye some'; and 'Bring in the coals an' ye'll a' get some'.

Sweets were a rarity in our house, but I remember, at the time of the South African War (the Boer War, as it was sometimes called) the lime flavour of boiled sweets, coloured green, which were sold as 'Lyddite Shells', named after a type of ammunition then in use.

Mother was particular about what we ate in the way of sweets; fruity sweets and boilings generally passed muster; anything pepperminty was acceptable, except chewing gum. The sweets we could afford cost under tuppence a quarter; luxury confectionery costing perhaps eightpence a quarter was quite beyond our contemplation.

At Christmas, and on other special occasions, we were, from time to time, presented with chocolate-coated sweets the size of a hazel-nut, containing a piece of preserved ginger, bars of Neapolitan Cocoanut Ice, Turkish Delight, smothered in fine powdery sugar, in drums of pale, thin wood, embellished with Eastern calligraphy, and Ferguson's tablet, in half-a-dozen pale colours and as many delicate flavours, and we agreed, with Wee Macgreegor, that 'taiblet is awfy guid'. Wee Macgreegor, typical Glesca laddie of his day (1903), was also fond of 'baurley sugar and gundy'; he had to behave, otherwise his mother threatened that he would not get carvies for his tea; and he was partial to soft sweets known as Hair Oil Mixtures, because their pleasant flavours were reminiscent of a barber's saloon.

The favourite sweets of Wishaw bairns were 'yelo-felos', small round balls like butter-nuts and, like many other bairns, they delighted in investing their Saturday Penny in a Lucky

Bag, which might contain a few sweets, a small toy, a tattie-gun, or a paper flower that opened out in water. Caroline remembers to this day the doll's mirror she got in her Lucky Bag, with tiny shells round it, and the gums and jujubes, jelly beans and jelly babies that were also available. Sweets that were slightly imperfect were generously handed out by shopkeepers for the Saturday Farthing, Ha'penny, Penny, or Tuppence, which was the extent of pocket-money in those days.

Some bairns got a stick of rhubarb to suck, occasionally dipped in a wee poke of sugar, or a piece of liquorice root, or a cut apple.

Town bairns at times got a slice of melon instead of sweets. They were sold in ha'penny slices. Afterwards, girls made necklaces of the seeds, washing them and drying them in the sun, before they began to string them.

James looks back on Saturdays in Dundee when 'my father took me round the Greenmarket and bought me a quarter of jaw-sticking almond gundy from the sweetie stalls lit by acetylene flares. Gundy was an auld farrant sweetie, much better than many of the toffees sold nowadays. It was made with brown sugar, butter and treacle, or golden syrup, with a flavouring of cinnamon; a hammer, or a flat iron, was needed to break it up.'

Malcolm calls to mind 'the days when we lived on an outlying sheep-farm in Peeblesshire. With my Saturday Penny I used to buy a very powerful sweet called Victory V gums, and cheap dates sold in a slab. I am now over sixty years old so it would appear that Winston Churchill did not invent the Victory V sign!'

'The very best buy I ever made with my Saturday Penny', Meg recalls with delight, 'was a miniature cardboard Bagatelle board with six numbered holes, six coloured balls, and two tiny cues. The balls and cues were of peppermint sugar. The little girl next door and I played all afternoon with them, and when we tired of the game we sat down and ate the cues!'

Maureen remembers that if you behaved yourself in church you got a pan-drop, but you had to be careful, for, if you bit it, it crunched and, if you sucked it, it made a rude noise and you got a 'red face', so it was best to let it slip soundlessly from

Pan–drops

cheek to cheek. Grown ups, who preferred an Extra Strong Peppermint lozenge for the sermon, would surreptitiously pass you that pan–drop. 'It is no longer a matter for stealth', she laughs, 'I know a little country place where it is the homely custom to offer them as you enter the church!'

There is an old Gaelic proverb which says 'Foolish is he who despises food', and leads us to more substantial ways of spending the Saturday Penny.

Elizabeth remembers when 'we used to go to the baker's shop in Tarland to buy a bag of "brokeners". These were broken biscuits of all sorts, butter biscuits, rice biscuits, parkins, and buttery heckle biscuits. Sometimes they were called "Broken Mixtures". They were a great treat and you got an awful lot for a penny. Funnily enough, I can't recall ever buying sweets.'

From Dinnet came the story of a Donside bairn in the late 1880s who was taken by her mother to Castle Newe (pronounced Nyow, to rhyme with cow). Lady Forbes gave

172

the child a round biscuit which she played with for a long time, rolling it along the table, but making no attempt to eat it. Her mother explained to Lady Forbes that her bairn had never before seen a biscuit, and thought it was a 'wheelie'.

Caroline has never forgotten the brandy wafers which the baker in Aberlour kept flat in an old-fashioned sweetie jar with straight sides. 'He sold them at four for a penny. His Abernethy biscuits were twice the thickness of those sold today. He also sold Paris Buns with crystallised sugar fragments on top, and German Biscuits, which were two thin rounds of shortcake, sandwiched together with jam, then iced on top and a cherry added for decoration. Towards the end of the First World War, owing to rationing restrictions, they lost their icing and their name. They became Empire Biscuits, a name they have retained ever since.'

'So many things I recall from hearing my aunt describe her early life', is how Elsie begins her story. 'After an illness she was sent to Aberdeen to stay with her Aunt Annie, who every day made her sit quiet in the Best Room with a glass of milk and "a fine piecie", sometimes it was a little cake, and sometimes it was thin bread and butter with carvies on it.' The latter was a 'great treat at teatime in many families', says Eleanor, 'The slice of buttered bread was held vertically and a spoonful of carvies (caraway seeds coated with white sugar) was sprinkled down the surface. They were in some places known as "seaside jam".'

Edward's favourite biscuits as a boy in Kilmarnock were made in the shape of mice with currants for eyes, and Cabin biscuits which were crackers made in pie-shells without the lid. These were mouthwatering when filled with butter and jam at tea-time.

One of Emma's happy childhood memories is of going to the baker from time to time 'where we could buy for threepence a large bag of Broken Pastries, lovely fresh cakes, cream buns, French cakes, jam tarts merely broken, and of Broken Biscuits we got about half a pound for a penny. Of spoiled fruit a ha'penny could buy a bagful . . . say, two apples, plums, a few cherries or a pear. Oranges were only seen at Christmas in those days.'

My father, as a boy in Laurencekirk, was fond of 'parlies'

which his mother used to make. They were a kind of gingerbread like parkins but bigger and thinner, which got their name from supposedly being popular with members of the Scottish Parliament. He also liked drop scones, the Scots pancake, which he loved to eat hot as they came off the girdle, without butter, jeely, or any other addition.

'Bawbee baps and Buttery Rowies' was an old Aberdeen street-cry. Baps are the traditional morning roll of Scotland.

Aberdeen is famed for its butteries and softies, two types of roll, and a pleasant memory for Margaret is of Aberdeen Morning Rolls delivered hot for breakfast, and only made in the Nor'East. 'They were not like bakers' baps,' she says, 'but were made with bakers' dough and butter, giving an almost flaky texture. In the Nor'East a bannock baked with a ring in it used to be given to a teething child to play with. When the bannock broke everyone present was given a small piece and the bairn used the ring as a teething ring.'

Forfar is well-known for its bridies, and Kirriemuir for gingerbread; Selkirk specialises in bannocks with fruit inside, and Dundee in shell pies and its world-famous Dundee Cake.

The contents of our poke at sorees in the Glen seldom varied – a softie, a bap, a cookie (a plain bun) and a cake. The cake could be one of several: a sponge-cake with a paper bandage round it, which gave it its name of a 'sair heidie', a triangle of shortbread called a petticoat tail (from the Petits Gateaux Tailles which Mary, Queen of Scots, brought from France) and a Queen Cake (which Mary did *not* bring over; these small cakes were not known till a later period) or a German Biscuit with a cherry on top.

Fife bairns loved the Jam Tit-Bits they were able to obtain before the First World War. They cost a penny each and were like large Butter Biscuits. Dumfries bairns, as a rule, preferred the crust of Black Bun, when it was fresh, to the rich fruit Bun itself. Shortbread, they declared, was nicer, if you could dunk it in your tea when nobody was looking. Large shortbread cakes appeared in Oughton's shop at Christmas. They had thick icing on them which was too hard to eat, lettered with sentiments like 'Lang may yer Lum Reek', 'Ye ken wha frae', and, for sending at New Year to overseas friends, 'Hands across the Sea'.

All seaweeds are rich in minerals. Carrageen Moss was said to be very good for chest complaints, containing, as it does, both iodine and sulphur.

'During the 1914 War', Flora recalls, 'we collected it on the shore at Stonehaven and used it as gelatine. It was light-coloured. Dulse was also an edible seaweed. The old way of preparing it was to place it, after cleaning, in an unbreakable container; then a poker was made red-hot in the fire and the dulse stirred with it till it was hot, then eaten. As for drinks, our favourites were American Cream Soda, Falkirk 'Irn Bru', and a concoction of lemonade made from yellow crystals.'

'Does anybody remember Iced Gems?' asks Sheila. 'They were tiny sugar-topped biscuits about the size of a sixpenny piece. Shirley Temple had Animal Crackers; we had biscuits iced with animal shapes as well as nursery-rhyme figures, and we had letters of the alphabet and animals in vermicelli which were very attractive in soup.'

When I was a baby, recovering from whooping-cough in Stirling, my Mother was advised by well-meaning friends to walk me round the gasworks; I doubt if she put much faith in gas-fumes as a tonic. In Glasgow, whooping children were sent out to sniff the tar-boilers in the street.

Apparently, children were unsympathetic to their suffering playmates, for Mary recalls a rhyme which said

> My father's a King,
> My mother's a Queen,
> I'm a little Princess
> And you're a dirty wee thing.
> Not because you're dirty,
> Not because you're clean,
> But because you've got the whooping-cough
> And measles in between.

When my children were convalescent from whooping-cough in the 1920s the doctor prescribed a dark brown liquid medicine which smelled and tasted of creosote. It was so unpleasant to take that one of the boys, aged about five at the time, dashed the spoon from my hand and splashed the horrid stuff on the bedroom wallpaper. The stain was for long a reminder of a brief and understandable act of rebellion.

When we were off-colour my Mother always gave us an egg beaten up in warm milk, sweetened. We loved it.

She believed in wrapping a woollen stocking round the neck at bedtime to relieve a sore throat, and had great faith in the efficacy of a bread-poultice. Many a time I sat with a finger wrapped in a large handkerchief which enclosed a soggy poultice . . . to draw out a thorn perhaps?

Ena had to wear a lump of camphor in a shot silk bag round her neck as protection during epidemics. It seemed to prove effective. She also had her chest rubbed with camphorated oil, and drops of camphor on a lump of sugar for colds.

'Who nowadays has heard of Dr Gregory's Mixture?' asks Grace. 'I have never lost my faith in it, and it is still possible to get it, mercifully in tablet form, in a chemist's shop in Dumfries. My mother seldom bothered to send for the doctor when she had good old Dr Gregory as a stand-by! She also had in her medicine-cupboard Ipecacuanha wine, Parrish's Chemical Food, and Brimstone and Treacle. Castor Oil was her remedy for all tummy upsets, and, like the Glesca keelie, we dreaded the prospect of having "to get ile".'

This seems a not inappropriate note on which to end a summary of the delights that were within the grasp of the proud possessor of a Saturday Penny!

Red Letter Days

Ma feet's cauld, ma shoon's thin,
Gie's ma cakes an' let me rin!

Of all the Red Letter Days in the Scots Calendar, Hogmanay, the last night of the year, is perhaps the most beloved.

'On the previous night', says Doreen 'an old custom is still carried on in Burghead. It is called "Carry Anchor", pronounced as one word, carrieanker. A long, strong stem of seawood is put in the oven to dry and toughen it. We used this to hammer on doors then ran for our lives lest we were caught. A friend who comes from Caithness has another version of this custom. He used a cabbage-stalk for his carrieanker. It was hollowed out, packed with hemp, and set on fire with a red-hot cinder. The smoke was blown through keyholes, and boys took to their heels when the door opened.'

Elizabeth remembers that 'At Hogmanay, every corner of our house was cleaned with frantic thoroughness; the ashes under the grate were emptied out, my Mother displayed her best tea-sets and bonnie jougies, and a crochet frill was tacked along the edge of the shelf.'

Helen recalls that 'In the morning, at Anstruther, children with baskets called at our door, saying, "Please, my cakes." We had ready a supply of Penticuits, specially made for Hogmanay by the local baker. They were rather dry, triangular biscuits with a blob of icing sugar on top. We also handed out oranges and coppers.

177

In St Monance, and a number of other places, bairns went round the shops and houses chanting

> Ma feet's cauld, ma shoon's thin,
> Gie's ma cakes an' let me rin!

But neither Maggie nor her friend Harriet was allowed to do this. Their parents considered it was begging, and declined to countenance it. 'When I was young, we sang at the doors of neighbours, but no farther afield. It didn't take us long to do our round; then we were off to bed early, because we hung our stockings up, hoping for more presents, tho' we had had the usual gifts at Christmas', says Jan.

'At Hogmanay in Brechin', Marjory recalls, 'both front and back doors were opened to let the New Year in and the old one out. Gamekeepers fired off their guns, and the Cathedral bells rang out at midnight. Crowds gathered at the Cross, and the Band played festive music, including "A Guid New Year tae ane an' a'"', ending with "Auld Lang Syne", after which everyone dispersed in order to First Foot their friends. Many continued without sleep throughout New Year's Day.

'The first of your First Footers had to be a dark man, if possible, to ensure Good Luck. Everyone took gifts when visiting on New Year's Day. *We* took kippers and smokies dressed as dolls in crepe paper! Shortbread and liquor were always acceptable.

'Christmas was not much celebrated in Scotland till about the end of the Second World War; in fact, there was no Public Holiday – shops and factories carried on as usual. New Year was the Great Celebration.'

Mary contributes a traditional song from the village of Sandend:

> Here begins a gweed New Year, be Souslem, be Souslem!
>   [by Jerusalem]
> Here begins a gweed New Year, an' awa' be Souslem Toon!
> Rise up, gweed–wife, an' shak' yer feathers,
> Dinna think that we are beggars,
> We're gweed bairnies come tae play,
> Rise up an' gie's wir Hogmanay!
> Wir feet's caul', wir sheen's thin,
> Gie's wir piece an' lat's rin!

The tod'll tak's afore we're deen,
An' awa' be Souslem Toon!
A bawbee an' a pucklie meal,
Be Souslem! Be Souslem!

Another Hogmanay rhyme was:

Blinken Jock the Cobbler, he had a blinken e'e,
He sold his wife for a hunder pun'
An' that wis a' his gear;
Wi' his pooches fu' o' siller
An' his barrel fu' o' beer,
Please tae help the guisers
An' we wish you a Happy New Year!

In numerous villages, children went out as guisers (that is, dis*guised*) and sang their version of the Hogmanay song, which might include:

Up sticks! Down stools!
Dinna think that we are fools!

and generally contained the line which exhorted the goodwife to rise up and shake her feathers, a reference to the daily necessity of shaking up a feather-bed.

'If Oor Hogmanay, in the shape of oranges, cakes, and coppers, was not immediately forthcoming', Malcolm reflects, 'little boys might shout:

Tramp, tramp, tramp, the boys are marchin'
We are the guisers at the door;
If ye dinna let us in, we'll bash yer doorie in,
An' ye'll never see the guisers any more!

Or the threat might be, "We'll smash yer windae in", but I have never heard that such a threat was ever carried out!

'About thirty years ago, on an outlying sheep-farm in Peeblesshire, my children and the shepherd's children decided to visit the nearest village dressed as guisers. Their ages would be between five and eleven. I well remember their return from the trip. They each had a sack and emptied the contents on the kitchen table. I was amazed at the quantity of food, fruit, and cash they had been given.'

In Edinburgh, the Guiser Play began soon after Hallowe'en

Guisers

180

and was carried on right up to Hogmanay. They planned to visit as many tenements as possible before the end of the year.

When I was very small, I was somewhat disturbed at my first sight of the guisers, who rang the bell for admission, and then came charging up the stairs with lowered heads, at each door revealing soot-blackened features, or masks, which they called their 'false faces'. They sang no song, but, clutching their pennies and sweeties, clattered away to their next objective.

'In Ballater, in the early 1890s, and possibly later', writes Mabel, 'the great excitement that night was the arrival of the village lads with blackened faces and wearing weird costumes, who called at every house to perform a traditional play, which had among its characters, Goloshan with his sword and pistol, Sir William Wallace, who "shed his blood for Scotland's rights", and "Good auld Dr Broon, the best auld doctor in the toon", who was asked "And what made *you* the best auld doctor in the toon?". His reply was "My travels, Sir.

> Hickerty pickerty hedgehog
> Three times round the West Indies
> An' back tae Auld Scotland again,
> I have gone from fireside to bedside." '

Flora quotes further lines from the Guiser Play:

> Here come I, Wee Keekum Funny,
> I'm the lad wha tak's the money.

In countless forms, this play is known all over Scotland and is of great antiquity.

At midnight in many towns, hooters and sirens made banshee noises, people danced in the streets and sang 'A Guid New Year tae ane an' a', An' mony may ye see', and the bells of Watch Night Services joined in. In Glasgow, in those days, every factory had its hooter to start and stop work, the main-line railway always had a good head of steam, and loud noises sounded upriver from the docks. It was all rather eerie.

'At midnight, in Anstruther', Helen says 'the herring boats blew their whistles, and in most houses in every corner of Scotland, the head of the house, rising from his chair at the first chime of the midnight hour, opened his front door to let the Old Year go out and the New Year come in, holding it open till "the last chap o' twelve", as a gesture of welcome.'

'Our table, in Fife, was spread with a white cloth, and laden with plates of home-made fruit-cake and shortbread, and Black Bun, rich and heavy with fruit and crust', sighs Elizabeth. 'My mother always made plenty of potted hough to make sandwiches for the First Footers who were our friends and neighbours. Bottles and glasses were at the ready. The first dark man to cross the threshold came bearing gifts representing Plenty in fuel, food and drink – a peat or a lump of coal, shortbread, and a bottle of something (in the old days it was whisky or ginger wine). We were allowed to stay up to see the First Foot arrive, and were glad to go to bed soon after, weary after the excitement of the day. We always had steak pie for New Year's dinner, and a clootie dumpling into which Mother had put charms. She always made a dumpling for Special Occasions throughout the year, like birthdays and family reunions.'

'At New Year Parties', Helen remembers, 'just before we went home we all sat on the floor in a semi-circle round the fire and we each got a puff, which was a triangular piece of pastry, very light and flaky, with jam in the middle.'

'Once a year', according to Robert, 'just after New Year, the Sunday School Soiree was held in the Church Hall. It was a Magic Lantern Show, and afterwards each child was given a poke of sweeties and an apple or orange. We used to bawl at the top of our voices

> How would you like to be me,
> And go to a Penny Soiree
> With a lump of fat stuck in my hat?
> How would you like to be me?'

Lizbeth's 'loveliest memory is of New Year which we always spent with my grandparents. Grandpa was famous in the village because of his Magic Lantern. We thought he was wonderful, as he certainly was, and we looked forward to his Lantern Show in his parlour for weeks beforehand. The fact that we saw mostly the same pictures every time made no difference; in fact we would have been most indignant if we had not seen our old favourites. Grandpa had even a moving picture – an old man with a snub nose which grew longer and longer, and there on the very tip sat a little mouse! How we loved that! We shouted, "Again, Grandpa! Again!" '

The First Monday in January was Handsel Monday when presents were given to celebrate the beginning of a new year in everything. 'I remember once my father gave me a bright new shilling for my Handsel' – a great event for Caroline!

'Shrove Tuesday was Brose and Bannock Day in Buckie', relates Flora, 'when children got a half-holiday from school. The mid-day meal consisted of Swede turnips boiled with a bone. When cooked and ready to serve, those who wanted brose before their neeps had a handful of oatmeal put in a basin, with salt and pepper added, and the boiling liquid from the neeps was poured over it. The mixture was stirred vigorously, then cooled a little before supping – a grand filler-up! The neeps were strained and mashed – a lovely meal when I was a youngster, over sixty years ago! Later that day a basinful of bannock or pancake mixture was prepared, and the batter fired on a girdle. I doubt if the youngsters of today have even heard of this ploy.'

'Shrove Tuesday was Rappy Nicht at Nether Dallachy', says Jessie. 'On our way home from school we collected yellow turnips complete with shaws, and carried them home. After dark we set off in groups and went to neighbours' doors, rapping a neep against the closed door. The master of the house came out and chased us away, and we ran skellickin' in pretended fear. This was the recognised procedure; householders entered into the fun. There was no more to it than this . . . rapping and skellickin!'

'Whuppity Scoorie' in Lanark on 1 March is a survival of a pagan festival, in which it is necessary to make a lot of noise to scare away evil spirits. Children still gather at six o'clock at the Cross, each holding a ball of paper tied with string. All the town dignitaries look on. When the old church bell is rung the children walk round the church three times swinging their paper balls. Then they have a mock battle hitting each other with the swinging balls. Later, pennies are thrown and bairns scramble for what they can find.

'Taillie Day was the last day of March when we tried to pin

paper tailies on each other', Dee recollects, 'even the grown-ups joined in. The tail had to be fixed without the victim's knowledge. Once I saw the minister going along the High Street with a lovely paper tailie on his back. He took it in good part when someone told him it was there.'

On 1 April we had to be careful to avoid 'Hunt the Gowk', to be on the alert for traps which playful adults set for guileless bairns. A gowk is a simpleton, and surely only a gowk could be taken in by the practical joker who persuaded him to deliver a letter marked URGENT, which contained only the words

> This is the first of Aprile,
> Send the gowk another mile!

And on he would be sent to yet another house, till some kind soul took pity on him, and maybe gave him an egg to his tea!

Rolling hard-boiled eggs at Easter appears to be still in vogue in many parts of Scotland; a favourite place in the old days for Edinburgh bairns was the daisy park between Joppa and Portobello. My sister and I ate our Hot Cross Buns among the daisies when we rolled our dyed eggs down a grassy slope, like the wee girl in the bairn-rhyme:

> I've got a smashin' Easter Egg,
> The brichtest ye hae seen,
> I'll tak it tae the Queen's Park
> An' rowe it on the green.
> I'll race it 'gainst the ither eggs
> An' tumble doun the brae,
> I warrant we'se hae lots o' fun
> An' ploys on Easter Day.
> An' when I'm tired o' rinnin' up
> An' doun, I'll rest a wee,
> An' gif my egg's no' tasht to bits
> I'll eat it for my tea!

'At Nether Dallachy', says Jessie, 'we gathered masses of whin blossom in our pinnies. The blooms were put in a big iron pot with water and brought to the boil on the open fire. Hard-boiled eggs were then put in the pot and they came out a nice yellow colour. We went round the village exchanging eggs with other children, and each ended up with a variety of colours as a few mothers used bought dyes; other mothers warned us that these might be dangerous to eat if there happened to be a crack in an eggshell. Dressed in our Sunday best we set off with our eggs, and some salt in a twist of paper, to the seaside where there was beautiful springy grass, and there we rolled our "Peace Eggs" on Easter Sunday. After they had been well and truly rolled, and collided many times with other eggs, we shelled and ate them, dipping them in the salt.'

In some parts of Shetland, as elsewhere, children collected their gifts of Pes Eggs (Pace or Pax). Elizabeth recalls that 'We all went to collect our "Paece Eggs" at the earnest request of our neighbours, whose hens, luckily, were beginning to "come in", that is, to lay. Children still do, but alas! the keeping of hens has dwindled, and eggs are very scarce in Bigton. We used to dye ours with tea-leaves, but dyeing was not a general practice.'

Emma has memories of Easter in Glasgow. 'Our eggs were hard-boiled, then Father dyed them with Condy's crystals, which made them either pale or dark purple. Our names were then put on with gold paint. Off to the park we would go to roll them down a hill. When they cracked, we shelled and ate them with bread and butter, with a drink of lemonade. That was our Easter Monday Treat.'

Rob, in his ninety-ninth year, has recalled an incident in his childhood and put it into verse:

> I wis jist an Aiberdeen laddie
> An' no' verra auld at that,
> Fan ma mither buskit me brawly
> In a gran' sailor suit an' straw hat.
>
> I wore it only on Sundays,
> 'Twis owre gran' for everyday wear,
> An' sure as roon cam' Monday
> It wis pitten awa' wi' care.
>
> Weel I min' o' that Easter Sunday,
> We a' wint doon tae the Links
> Tae row oor eggs on the Braid Hill,
> My wird! Bit we had rare jinks!

Fan we wis ready for hame
Disaster struck tae oor dismay,
A guff o' win' cam owre the Links
An' carried ma straw hat away.

We ran but we cudna catch it,
It skippit clean oot o' sicht,
Ma braw sailor hat wis lost,
I grat sair, as weel I micht.

Wi' heavy herts we made for hame,
But ere we gained the street,
Up cam' a quine wi' ma sailor hat,
Sayin' 'Here's yer hat, loon, dinna greet!'

A've ne'er seen that lass sin syne,
But I bless her 'til this day,
For her kindly words tae a puir wee loon
Whase sailor hat hid blawn away.

Alena's mother told her many a time how she and her school-friends used to celebrate Queen Victoria's Birthday with a bonfire and fireworks. They sang

The Twenty-fourth of May
Is the Queen's Birth-Day,
If we dinna get a holiday
We'll all run away!

But they did get a holiday! With the wood and odds and ends they had collected and hoarded for weeks, they made bonfires, and grown-ups joined in the fun.

Jessie recalls with affection the Annual Picnic. 'Everybody in the village contributed towards the cost, and a piper from a neighbouring village piped us all to the Howe Moss . . . there were young mothers pushing prams, old people with their staffs, and all the bairns carrying paper flags and bags of buns. Everybody was in gala mood. A big copper urn had been borrowed from the school, and willing helpers were already on the spot with a good fire going and boiling water ready for the brewing of tea. My father had put up shoogs on the high trees the previous evening, with stout salmon ropes, all the men in the village being salmon-fishers. We bairns never tired

186

of the swings; we ran races, had tugs of war and other exciting things to amuse us, and, as far as I recall, it was always a lovely day. When the bairns had tired, and the old folk had gone home, the young men and girls arrived for the dancing. A man with an accordion and another with a fiddle played for this, and a dancing-board was set up on a level piece of ground. They danced quadrilles, lancers, Strip-the-Willow, the Eightsome Reel and waltzes. Such laughter and happiness and such simple fare!'

Elsie's happy memories of other days include a stage-coach outing to Glen Esk. 'The owner of the coach had retired from his regular route to Edzell and Brechin, but he turned out for this occasion . . . a picnic was planned. We had all to get out at a steep hill to let the horses have a rest and a drink of water. There were in those days troughs at the roadside streams to provide horses with a much-needed drink after a long haul. We piled in again when we got to the top.'

Here is Edith's account of a memorable Sunday School Picnic in July 1901: 'The sun was shining brightly and the Borderland looked beautiful. We had been told by our teachers to meet at the church-door, so there I was, an excited eight-year-old with my tinnie tied round my neck. I wore a stiffly-starched white muslin frock with matching hat which had a wide brim stiff with starch. Our marvellous transport arrived – three lorries drawn by cart-horses decked with brightly-coloured ribbons and rosettes. One by one we were swung up to perch on forms placed back to back on the lorries. No Rolls Royce could have matched those lorries for glamour! We had a triumphal journey through the town of Galashiels, cheered on by the townspeople, and along the Melrose Road to Elwyn Glen and our picnic field, with its little bridges spanning a burn. Teachers put up swings on the old trees and we swung higher and higher among the leafy branches. Tea followed. Like gold-diggers we explored the contents of our pokes . . . no crisps, no sausage-rolls, no sandwiches in those days – just a cookie, a London bun, a biscuit and, to crown all, an iced cake!

'Later, we ran races . . . first prize, a penny, and a sweet to each of the other competitors. We played games like "Nuts in May" and "The Farmer's in his Den", and all too soon it was

187

time to go home, but we looked forward to the fun of the return journey on the lorries. Alas! before we reached home, down came the rain – a regular downpour! My starch was the first apparent casualty. As the starch dissolved my muslin frock became a sodden mass, and my hat-brim, which was my pride and joy, became softer and softer and lower and lower. I travelled back through the town unseen and unseeing behind the remains of my famous brim . . . truly pride goes before a fall!'

Henry remembers an occasion when a crowd of little girls, who had been invited to play in his mother's garden, could not resist the temptation to 'tummle the cat' down a steep grassy bank in the rose garden . . . a ploy which brought forth the stern admonition from the nun in charge: 'Only gurrls with closed draa'rs may somersault down the bank.'

Jack's most vivid memories as a wee laddie are of trips doon the watter [the River Clyde] and of the strawberry-picking Season at Blairgowrie, to which we all looked forward. That was a time when Blairgowrie's population was doubled, and there were tents, and huts, and caravans everywhere . . . this at a time when these were seldom seen . . . long before caravanning became popular. As Belle Stewart puts it:

> When berry-time comes roond each year
> Blair's population swells,
> There's every kind o' picker there. . . .
> A' flock tae Blair at berry-time
> The straws an' rasps tae pick. . . .
> Ye'll traivel far afore ye'll find
> A kinder lot than they. . . .
> I bless the hand that brocht me
> Tae the berry-fields o' Blair.

'Good shows came to our town. We used to go to a show in the Town Hall and our price to get in was a jam-jar', George tells us. 'The Band of Hope was one of the great events of the week. Every Friday our Church Hall was packed, and the Superintendent conducted a kind of Variety Performance. Sankey's Hymns, Temperance choruses bawled with uninhibited verve, duets, solos and recitations were rendered and applauded, especially when the performer was your own pal!

Band of Hope

189

Then came the main event of the evening – a talk by a local celebrity or popular speaker. Sometimes there would be illustrations on the blackboard; once we were thrilled to hear a gramophone, and on really big occasions there would be a limelight magic-lantern. On the closing night of the season we had a "soree" . . . tea, with a poke containing a bun, a cookie, and a cake; terrific enthusiasm, a special programme . . . how we revelled in it all!

'These events were, at times, linked with the Sunday School, and prizes were given for good work. I still treasure my first award.

'Sometimes we were invited to choose our closing hymn; the shout would go up "Dare to be a Daniel", not altogether because of the rousing tune, but because that was the Church Officer's name, and he would be within hearing waiting to lock up. When you come to think of it, the words of the chorus were not inappropriate!

> Dare to be a Daniel,
> Dare to stand alone,
> Dare to have a purpose firm,
> Dare to make it known.'

'A great event in the summer at Anstruther was the Sunday School Trip', Helen recollects. 'We went in decorated corn-carts. The horses, too, were decorated with ribbons, and were driven by ploughmen in their Sunday suits to a big field on a farm about two miles away. Our picnic lunch consisted of tuppeny meat pies and lemonade in the old-fashioned bottles with the glass marbles in the neck, which you pressed down with your thumb. We ran races and later had milk, tea, and buns.'

Also from Elsie: 'The great place for singing games was our Sunday School Trip. Before we got sophisticated and had a special train to take all the Sunday Schools in the town to Broughty Ferry, the trip was usually held in a neighbouring farmer's field. We took part in many familiar singing-games, like "Nuts in May" which was very popular because a large number of players was available. The two long lines advanced and retired, singing the well-known verses. When it came to the question, "Who will you send to take her away?" we sent a boy; if a boy had been chosen, we sent a girl to take him away; then came the tug-of-war, and one or the other joined the opposite side.'

'In the twenties and early thirties, on a certain day in June', Marjory tells us, 'we assembled in our prettiest summer dresses and proceeded to the picnic spot in the Mearns, perched on lorries drawn by heavy Clydesdale horses with decorated harness. They were lent for the occasion by local carriers, coal-merchants, and dairymen. At the picnic spot we ran races, and men and boys had tugs-of-war. We girls had skipping through an enormous rope (very painful if you missed your jump)! We were issued with strong tea from an urn, and got a pokie containing a scone, a cake, and a biscuit. I don't remember if there was lemonade . . . there was certainly no ice cream. We used to go about three miles, singing all the way, with the horses' harness jingling.'

'The Sunday School Picnic in Gourdon was held on a Saturday', Louisa remembers. 'We went in procession, headed by the Village Band, from the school to the sea-greens. Aunt Sally was a great attraction, her wooden figure dressed in old clothes, with a clay pipe in her mouth. Bundles of sticks were handed out. You stood at a distance and threw sticks to see how many pipes you could break. The picnic food was brought to the spot from the baker's shop in a horse-drawn lorry. We ran the usual races . . . egg-and-spoon, thread the needle, three-legged, and wheelbarrow (one boy walked on his hands, his partner held him up by his legs and directed him). We also plaited the Maypole.'

Mabel relates that 'Lorries were decorated for the Sunday School Trip to one of the many castles in the vicinity of Brechin – Brechin Castle, Kinnaird Castle, Careston Castle. Forms were tied on the lorries on which we children sat. The carter walked beside his horse and led it. We were conducted through the grounds but were never inside the castle. A field was allocated for games and races. Kinnaird Castle was said to have as many windows as there are days in the year, and we were told that the young Earl was very daring, and had traversed the face of the castle, springing from one window-ledge to another.'

From Castle Douglas there were Sunday School Trips to

nearby farms, in box-carts with high wooden frames, and big wooden wheels with iron rims which could draw sparks from the dusty roads. They were drawn by heavy-footed Clydesdales with their tails and manes pleated and be-ribboned for the occasion; these were marvellous outings. At one time races were organised round the village of Gelston, with contestants wearing fancy dress, and excitement assured from start to finish.

And here is Jean's Jaunt! 'In Forfar, the summer highlight was the Jaunty, the name we gave to the Sunday School Jaunt. We were taken in horse-drawn brakes to a field a couple of miles away, and when the sun shone it was a day to remember!'

'I remember', says Muriel, 'the thrill of driving to a town, and riding on the top of an open tram, and swinging the top of the seat across so that we, all four, sat as a group. It was nearly an annual outing, and a real highlight.'

'We sat on straw on the way to our Sunday School Picnic', says Jane. 'My tinny was slung round my neck on a ribbon, and we had paper streamers to play with. I remember the white frock I was wearing, a white ribbon in my hair, blue sash, black hand-knitted stockings and black button-boots. I was seven.'

'We didn't have a bathroom in our house', Elizabeth tells us, 'but a school-friend and I had a tub-wash in the wash-house, with A1 soap-powder and Parazone in the water, no Lux soap for us! We went to the Picnic in Kennoway in a nice clean dress, a tinny tied with a ribbon like a sash, and a handkie to wave from the train. What cared we if it rained? We always had a grand time, especially in the train!'

A ride in a train 'by your lane' was also a wonderful experience, as this charming poem suggests.

Awa' tae Dundee

I'm seven year auld,
And I'm awa' tae visit ma auntie at Dundee,
I'm awa' tae visit ma auntie Elspet,
Her that's named for me.

Aince we're owre the Forth Brig I'll be gettin'
  ma tea
Oot o' a wee pot a' tae masel.
An' a milk-jug, tae.
There's a man in the white coat roarin' alang the
  corrie-door,
'Any more for tea, any more for tea?'
Just as he's gaun past, I cry on him,
'Aye, there's *me*.'
He looks at me like a muckle dug lookin' at a wee
  yin.
'My! My! I didna ken we had the Queen
  traivellin' the day,
Come awa' an' get yer tea.'
Doon I sit in the dinin'-caur, wi' ma braw reid
  bag on the table,
Sae that they can a' see,
An' the white coat serves me, afore them a'!
An' I get a toastit tea-cake tae ma tea.
There I sit as mim as a puddock
Till we get tae Dundee,
Then I'm no' a queen ony mair,
I'm jist wee Elspet gettin' oot o' the train,
An' there's ma auntie on the platform,
Her that's named for me
                    (Meg Marshall, by kind permission)

I remember when the Diamond Jubilee of Queen Victoria
was celebrated in every part of her Empire. There was a
procession through London on 22 June 1897, the hottest day in
a very hot summer, followed by a fête in Hyde Park when
30,000 children had a feast of buns and lemonade, with games
and prizes, and the Queen herself helping to distribute
souvenir mugs. We, in the Glen, also had a procession, from
the School to the Haugh of Tamnafeidh, and a fête, which was
called a picnic, with tea served to everyone seated on the grass,
with a cup in one hand and a poke containing buns in the other.
Women in their Sunday best made the tea, and men carried
round the big tin tea-pots. Every child was presented with a
souvenir mug, even the Manse baby, one month old, whose

193

feeding-bottle was heated that day by immersion in the large urn in which tea for the multitude was prepared over a wood fire. There were games and races for the children, dancing for all to the music of the pipes on a board set up on the grass, and a grand show of fireworks to round off the day.

I also recall that we had two picnics to celebrate King Edward VII's coronation. The buns and cakes had already been ordered for celebrating the coronation that had to be postponed because the King was ill, so it was decided to hold the picnic as arranged. Then we had another on the actual Coronation Day. I recall being piped in a procession to the picnic place where there were the usual games and dancing.

'I was brought up very frugally in Banffshire', says Flora, 'We had no "loaf bread" as the old people called it, and when we got tired of oatcakes we used to break them up and crumble the meal through our fingers into a bowl of milk, and sup it with a spoon. Another dish which had oatmeal in it was "skirlie", of which we were very fond. The meal was fried in bacon fat till it was all absorbed, and we ate it so hot it nearly burned our mouths. "Soor dook" was the name our parents gave to buttermilk, which we all considered a very refreshing drink.'

'Our only Fair was once a year and was the highlight of our school holidays. This was Peter Fair, or Rathven Market. It was held in a field some miles from our home, so it meant a long walk there and back. We didn't have much spending-money, and a penny was a fortune! It was partly a Horse and Cattle Market, and partly a Fun Fair. Only the Fun Fair has survived.'

'Feeing Markets were when the agricultural workers came in to Brechin twice a year, in May and November', explains Marjory, 'to seek new jobs or to be re-engaged. They stood around in the High Street and struck bargains with the farmers. Down each side of the High Street and Market Street were stalls and roundabouts and coconut shies. In June there was a larger assembly called Taranty Fair, originally a horse-trading market. It has now become a two-day Fun Fair with the usual amusements and the Fair people come from a wide area. As children, we always got a box of sweets on Market Days.'

'A Red Letter Day for us school-boys in Dumfries', says Roy, 'was the Rood Fair held in the autumn, featuring roundabouts and sideshows. One I shall always remember was the Joy Wheel, a circular dais of polished wood, on which we had all to sit, in a huddle, facing outwards. The Wheel revolved at ever-increasing speed, boys and girls sliding off in all directions, with an astonishing display of underwear, until the last one was flung off.'

Edward describes a typical fairground in his boyhood: 'at the entrance a wide passage was made between barrows and stalls selling fruit and sweets and bits of coconut, the women in charge shouting their wares:

Cocoa-Nit

A bawbee a bit!

'There was a stall in the Fun Fair where a glass case was fixed. Inside it was one of the early phonographs. It had cylinder records. This was long before the gramophone with HMV disc records became popular. Outside the glass case were rubber tubes like those on a doctor's stethoscope. You paid a penny and chose a record from the list, and the sound came through the tubes. In a very squeaky voice came the usual introduction, "This is an Edison Bell Record", and you heard a song or a band.

'There were swing-boats and shooting-galleries, and "hairy marys" to be knocked back at three shots a penny, with a coconut or a woolly monkey on a stick as the prize. There were trays of gey cheuch gundy, gingerbread horses, and dollops of sticky dates for sale, and all the cheap knick-knacks that were hawked round country fairs.

'We went to all the Feeing Fairs, like the Marymass Fair at Irvine, and the Curd and Grosset Fair at Kilmarnock. Curds and grossets were laid out on a long table. The man in charge of the curds flourished a long knife, and cut off what was required from a great big chunk. Slabs of French Nougat, Lotus Toffee, and peppermints were also on sale.'

Lindsay remembers the men and buxom lassies who were lined up to be looked over by the farmers and their wives. 'It was like a cattle-market! The farmers felt the muscles of the men and noted if they had a healthy glow and straight backs; what the wives were looking for in the lassies I couldn't guess.'

The Annual Timmer Market at Aberdeen had a great reputation in its heyday, but lost much of its former glory when the demand for hand-made wooden articles gave way to a craving for plastic fairings. Still, there was All the Fun of the Fair for us bairns, and for the laughing lads and lasses.

Louisa recalls that 'At Bervie there used to be a Cattle Market in the Spring, where cattle were brought from near and far to be sold. There was no auctioneer. A man simply stated a price for his beast, and that was that – take it or leave it! There were travelling shows, and tables laid out with Gingerbread Men and Gingerbread Horses; we all got some.'

Ena remembers that 'Once a year a small Fair stopped at Nithsdale on its way to join the Big Fair at Dumfries, but we were not supposed to go to it in case we caught germs or fleas, which were rife in those days.'

We had few formal treats, and those were enjoyed in anticipation and long after they were a thing of the past. Such an event was Bostock and Wombell's Menagerie, which pitched its tents one summer day on a grassy strip on a bank of the River Dee near Ballater.

We walked five miles to visit it, and, having paid threepence each for admission, wandered round the cages to look at the pathetic wild animals. Only the elephants were uncaged, and they were paraded round the big marquee giving rides to venturesome bairns. I was shocked to the depths of my little Puritan soul when a keeper shouted, "Stand Clear! Ladies and Gentlemen! All those who cannot swim . . . the Big Elephant is about to make his water!" Small boys who lacked the price of admission peered under the tent-flaps till chased away by irate showmen. The show was on a very modest scale, but we thought it well worth the money . . . in high spirits we chased each other round the outside of the big grey tents, jinking under guy-ropes before setting out on the long trek home.'

Margaret tells us a delightful story! 'In the park near us in summertime, there were bands playing in the bandstand, and most nights a group of entertainers were there. Of course, we had no money to pay for seated accommodation, so we used to stand at the railing and poke our noses through. We had to get there very early to get a place right next to the railing, and so be able to see clearly. Incidentally, about a year ago, I wanted to take ciné shots of Glasgow Parks, and in Kelvingrove Park, near where I used to live, there was a children's entertainment on, and there, at the railings, were five small children with their noses poked through to be as near as possible to the scene. Remembering my childhood I asked them if they would like to go into the seats; the rapture on their faces was touching, so I bought them tickets . . . a small amount. They were barely seated . . . I went in with them . . . when they kept looking back to the entrance, and I discovered that they had arranged to meet two friends, and there they were, at the railings! I gave them money to pay for their friends' admission, and for that modest outlay I had one of the happiest experiences of my life. It made me feel like a millionaire, or, as a friend remarked, a Fairy Godmother!'

Jamie's mouth waters when he describes the Annual Berry Picnic at the Manse when every Sunday School scholar received a large mugful of nice juicy red grossets!

Dorothy regrets she cannot complete the couplet chanted by bairns in the Cowgate district of Edinburgh when returning from their Annual Sunday School Picnic, between the years 1914 and 1920. It went

> Back tae Edinburry once more,
> That's the toon that I adore.   [See note, p. 206]

Elsie recalls that in addition to the Sunday School Trip there was the Cloan Outing, which was a long-established institution, originally promoted in the interests of temperance, when the Haldane Family invited all the school-children to a picnic in a field behind the House of Cloan. This was nearly two miles from Auchterarder, up a steep hill, and there was no means of transport. 'We probably assembled at the school and all marched up together', she remarks, 'but I only remember going, with my tinny on a ribbon round my neck, with my mother who often told me that at one time the children feasted on baps and rhubarb jam, but we got a pasty, a cookie, and a Paris bun. Lady Haldane organised the games and races, and while the girls had singing-games the boys were kicking a ball about.'

'In Winter,' Helen narrates, 'there was the Church Soiree for both adults and children, which was held in the church because there was no hall. As we entered we each were handed a cup and saucer and a poke which contained a cookie, a bun, a sugar cake, and a piece of shortbread. The young ladies of the congregation went round with brass kettles to pour out tea. The communion table was spread with a white cloth and a proper tea was laid for the visiting ministers who were to be the speakers. They also got fruit, and I rather envied them sitting there consuming grapes, almonds and raisins between the speeches.'

We often heard of the wonders of the cinematograph but never attended such an entertainment. I do remember a magic-lantern show provided by a generous lady, when the operator acted as commentator, reciting for our benefit the substance of the stories pictured on the crudely-coloured lantern-slides. They were mainly about little crossing-sweepers who warmed their blue-with-cold hands at burning braziers, little girls who sold flowers in the street and pleaded 'Won't you buy my pretty flowers?', and a particularly harrowing story of a little match-seller who struck her matches one by one in an effort to keep warm but was found next morning lying frozen in the snow, her last match gone.

George remembers that sometimes a missionary would give a magic-lantern show (with half the slides put in upside down at first) or show an improving tale on film, like 'Jessica's First Prayer'; and Elsie gleefully relates how the New Year concert given by local talent was always very popular, but the year that a Glasgow concert party was engaged was considered to be a flop. 'Once, a theatrical party came', she concludes, 'I had never seen make-up before and thought them very low!'

I was very small when I was taken to a Carnival in the Waverley Market, where a woman lion-tamer put her head sideways into a lion's mouth and smiled at us from under its huge teeth! and to Poole's Entertainment for Children, in the Synod Hall, where paintings were moved across the stage on rollers and we were transported on a Lightning World Tour!

'When I was a wee laddie', says Lindsay, 'I was taken to my first circus on a Saturday; next day, I was taken to church for the first time and, halfway through the service, I piped up to Dad, "When is the clown comin' on".'

'A Red Letter Day in my life was in Perth in 1909 or 1910, when I remember seeing the wonder of a comet in the sky in the early evening – an astonishing sight! Seeing my first aeroplane was another highlight! Cody came to Lanark in 1910. My Dad went up with him in his flying-machine on one of his ten-bob-flips. The machine as I remember it, was a string and cane contraption . . . but it flew!'

My first ride in a motor-car took place in Stirling in 1897. In those days such an outing contained an element of adventure. As we drove along the roads outside the town the hedges were white with dust which rose in clouds. We were not critical of the speed; we were travelling on the level just as fast as the horses we were accustomed to sit behind, and, going downhill, nothing could pass us!

Elsie recalls a Sunday School party 'when we had the usual run of singing-games, Bobbie Bingo, Wally, Wally, Wall-flowers, and so on. The new Superintendent, a Glasgow-based Englishman announced, "Now we'll play Lubin Loo" and had us all flummoxed. He was met with blank stares, until a teacher, a pawky Scot, called to us, "Ach, it's Hally-go-lee!" and *that* we could understand; so we sang with enthusiasm:

> Hally-go-lee-go-lum,
> Hally-go-lee-go-light,
> Hally-go-lee-go-lum
> Upon a Saturday night!

The game proceeded as for the better-known Lubin Loo, with a loud Hooch at the end of every verse. It has now been modernized into the hilarious Hokey Cokey.'

One of the big events of the year was the 'Meal an' Ale', or Kirn Supper, held after the harvest was safely gathered in. Village children were all invited, and loved to sup basinfuls of cream crowdie, sometimes called 'fro' milk', which had the flavour and consistency of whipped cream. Meal and Ale, which gave its name to the Harvest Home, was really a kind of crowdie. A large basin was filled with home-brewed ale, treacle was added to sweeten it, and handfuls of oatmeal stirred in. It was always prepared in the morning to allow the meal to be absorbed, and 'a good sup whisky' was stirred through it. It was served at the end of the evening feast in the barn, and a ring was put in the mixture. Whoever found it would be the first to be married . . . so they said! Bakers in Fife made 'Shearers Scones' at harvest-time like large baps. They must also have been made for gangs of hungry workers at the time of sheep-shearing, and so got their name.

Helen recalls that 'on the first Monday in October the Anstruther herring fleet went off to Yarmouth for the herring-season there. Bakers baked large, very hard biscuits for the men to take with them, as bread would have gone stale on the long trip. We children used to go down to the pier to see them go off, and wait hoping to have biscuits thrown up to us.'

Doreen recalls that, at Hallowe'en, children in Elgin, dressed as guisers, used to go round the streets crying

Eelie, Eelie, Ollie,
Gie's nits, gie's nits [give us nuts],

a cry that has not come to light in any other district.

Schoolboys in Elgin prior to the First World War celebrated the evening before Hallowe'en as 'Batter-door-Nicht'. Every boy armed himself with a kail runt, that is, the heavy stalk with root attached that was left in the ground when the kail leaves were picked. 'We formed a long line at one end of the street', says Alex, 'and at a given signal we started to run along the street, each boy battering at every door with the runt. It was mostly taken in good part and looked on by householders as harmless fun, but some irascible people would come out and chase us. Once I had a bucket of water thrown over me.'

> First come the kirn-feast,
> Neist Hallowe'en;
> I got mysel' a muckle neep
> Frae Farmer Broon yestreen.
> I'll hollow oot the inside,
> Mak' flegsome e'en and mou'
> Pit in a lichted caunle
> To gie them a' a grue.
> We're ready noo for guisin',
> An' a' the friendly folk
> Gie aipples, nits, and siller
> To fill the guiser's poke.

We'll feenish up at my hoose
Doukin' in a byne,
And eatin' champit tatties,
Like auld land syne.

The turnip lantern is a survival of the days when no one dared venture out-of-doors after dark without a lantern to scare the witches who, with other evil spirits, were abroad at Hallowe'en.

Malcolm remembers how 'we raided many a hill-farmer's fields, and hacked a neep on the top of a gate-post, letting the moisture run down our chins as we bit deep into the juicy texture. They were sweeter than apples, to be compared only with the scraping of the jelly-pan when my mother had been making jam.'

In Banff they 'howkit oot a neep, wi' glowerin' e'en an' great big teeth, an' a penny caun'le for a licht.'

Jan describes how in Broughton they spent days beforehand in preparations, making lanterns by hollowing the neeps out carefully, leaving only a hollow stump to hold the candle which would glow eerily through the fearsome face they had cut out; 'assembling our costumes, and burning corks so that we could blacken our faces. We called ourselves tramps, not guisers, and felt sure that, with our black faces and trampish clothes, we would frighten everybody. No traditional folksy songs for us! What *we* sang outside front doors was 'You are my Sunshine, my only Sunshine!' Nevertheless, we were generously rewarded with cakes, fruit, and money. When it came to teatime, we got champit tatties, very light and fluffy, beaten up with butter and very hot milk, with maybe a spoonful of cream; and a clootie dumpling made rich with lots of currants, sultanas, and spice. Both champers and dumpling had charms in them.'

'We had bobbin' for apples at Portsoy,' Mary remembers, 'trying to spear them with a fork from the height of a chair as they bobbed about in a tub of water; and to bite them, with hands held behind our backs, as they dangled by a string from the rafters. We got very sticky faces when we tried to bite the treacle-smeared scones which were also suspended from the rafters.'

Hallowe'en neeps

'Dookin' for Aipples' the traditional way in Newmilns was to have ready a galvanised bath half-filled with water. Each child knelt by the tub in turn, and (protected, if need be, with a towel) tried to seize one of the bobbing apples with his teeth. If he did not succeed after three attempts, it was the turn of the next child. Or a chair was placed with its back against the tub. Each child then took it in turn to kneel on the chair and, holding a fork between his teeth, tried to spear an apple by dropping the fork on it. Sometimes a child was permitted to stand on the chair, and drop the fork by hand.

They had champers in Dumfries – creamed potatoes which were ladled out and found to contain charms such as were usually found in the Christmas Pudding.

> Min' hoo we dooked for aipples then?
> The traikle scones, an' ging'bread men?
> An' chestnuts roastin' in the grate
> By jumpin' oot wad tell's oor fate?

In Shetland villages, most of the boys went guising, dressed in hat and cloak elaborately made of straw and decorated with ribbons. They were called 'skeklers' and set out singly or in pairs. They collected pennies and in the evening they and the girls met in one house or another, where a party was provided from the proceeds of the collecting-tin, and a savoury supper with chappit tatties and neeps was served.

An old body in her hundredth year, in Aberdeen, used to recite

> Hallowe'en ae nicht at e'en,
> Three witches tae be seen,
> Ane black an' twa green,
> An' a' cryin' 'Hallowe'en!'

Other seasonal rhymes were:

> Holy on a cabbage-stock,
> Holy on a bean,
> Holy on a cabbage-stock,
> The morn's Hallowe'en,

and:

> Hallowe'en, ae nicht at e'en
> I ha'rd an unco squeakin',
> Doleful Dumps hed gotten a wife,
> They ca'd her Jenny Aitken!

Robert says 'We used to recite the following rhyme:

> Hallowe'en is here,
> It comes but once a year,
> Apples rosy red
> Float in the water clear.
> Hold the fork on high — drop it —
> Hi! *You've* got a big one!'

'We children in Angus went out guising in fancy dress', Marjory relates, 'going from house to house in the neighbourhood. We were rewarded after singing and reciting to our hosts. At home, after the fun of Dookin' for Apples was over we sat round a huge dish of delicious stovies, which had cooked very slowly on the top of the stove in a covered pan, with salt and pepper and knobs of butter. Threepenny bits and charms were hidden in the stovies. Afterwards, we sat round the fire and told ghost stories.'

I remember being told by some aged cottage-folk near Balmoral how for long it was the custom to make torches of splintered pine, and every man, woman, and child able to carry a burning brand ran round the boundaries of their homes at midnight, so protecting themselves and their possessions from wicked spells until next Hallowe'en. It was wonderful, they said, to be on a hillside that night and to see all the flickering lights moving round the homesteads in the valley.

This torch-bearing custom greatly interested Queen Victoria when she lived at Balmoral, as she did for a great part of each year of her life. She used to watch, and even join in the procession of torch-bearers which paraded the Castle boundaries. The final scene was very spectacular. They threw all the blazing torches in a heap, added more pinewood to make a bonfire, and by its light, danced Highland Reels to the music of the bagpipes. In one reel the men held flaming torches high over their heads while they danced. It must have been an amazing sight!

The Fifth of November, Guy Fawkes' Day, was not reckoned as a special date for Scots bairns till after the First World War, but in many towns it is now used as an excuse for letting off more squibs and bangers.

Ena recalls: 'What happy parties we had in Winter. After doing justice to the good things on the laden table (set with my Grandmother's china, which is still intact) including Cheese Pudding, followed by scones and cream cookies, we played charades. My Aunt had chests of old Victorian dresses and parasols, and some terribly funny masks of old men and women. First, the young people would act, then our elders. There was never any idea of segregating the age-groups. Later, some of the members of the family who were away at the War, in 1914 and later, came home on leave, and some never again.'

'As we grew older,' says Effie, 'we found charades great fun, and also dressing up in all sorts of clothes which were kept in an old trunk. We invented Music Hall "turns" to perform to an audience of all the grown ups who could be pressed into attending.'

Emily remembers when indoor games at parties were competitive and a forfeit was demanded of the loser. A handkerchief, a bracelet or a brooch were collected and retained in a basket till the end of the games when an adult or older child would sit blind-folded and select from the basket each item in turn, chanting: 'Here is a thing, a very pretty thing, what's to be done with the owner of this pretty thing?' The owner might be asked to bite an inch off the poker, which left the victim non-plussed till it was explained that the poker could be held an inch away from his face; or he might be instructed to 'kneel to the prettiest, bow to the wittiest, and kiss the one you love best'. Other penalties were to 'call your sweetheart's name up the chimney' (there was always a chimney in those days), to 'kiss all the flowers on the carpet' (suddenly all the girls sat down on the floor), and a Rabbit Kiss was when a boy and a girl at each end of a piece of string had to chew their way along it till they met in the middle and kissed.

'Elaborate teas were set on individual tables lit by little lamps', Margaret remembers. 'Soft drinks were from syphons which added colour and sparkle. There were sandwiches, sausage-rolls, cakes, jellies, trifles, and sometimes ice-cream. There were little dishes of sweets on the tables, among them "reading sweeties" and at the end of the tea-party these flew thick and fast between tables. Party fare was much appreciated . . . home fare was for most of us "plain and wholesome".'

Indoor games for winter evenings, in childhood days, can only be mentioned in passing. Ludo, Snakes and Ladders, draughts and dominoes, pencil and paper games like 'Consequences', and card-games like 'Happy Families' are still with us. Party games were mainly 'Spin the platter', 'Hunt the thimble', guessing games, and 'The Queen of Sheba'.

'Once a year, for a special treat', Elsie recollects, 'we were taken to Hengler's Circus which came every Winter to Sauchiehall Street in Glasgow. Outside the theatre stood women wrapped in voluminous woollen shawls, with heavy baskets of oranges on their arms. Their cries of 'Sweet Seville Oranges, three a penny!' filled us with excitement and anticipation, for oranges were only to be had at Christmas. Inside, the theatre was already filled with the aroma of oranges . . . that, and the sound of the orchestra tuning up, were part of the thrilling atmosphere.

'When the usual circus acts were over then came the scene

205

that surpassed everything – the Water Scene! The stage seemed to dissolve and an enormous waterfall appeared, and a loch surrounded by rocks and trees. This, curiously, was the setting for a Cowboys and Indians scene. There was a lot of shooting which we enjoyed, though at times it was a little alarming; but our parents were with us and we were not really afraid. Good old Hengler's! Alas, it has gone!'

Note

The Grassmarket 'Barrie's Trip' is recalled at this point, and further lines from the chant of the Cowgate bairns are remembered:

> Back tae auld Edinburry once more,
> That's the toon that I adore,
> And I hope tae see,
> And I hope tae be,
> In auld Edinburry once more.

Glossary

aa, all
aald, old
ablow, below
ahin, ahint, behind
atween, between
auld farrant, old-fashioned
Auld Lang Syne, days of long ago
ava, at all
averins, cloudberries

bake, biscuit
baps, yeasted rolls eaten all over
   Scotland
barra, barrie, wheelbarrow
bawbee, halfpenny
beck an' boo, nod and bow
begood, began
black sugar, liquorice stick
blaeberries, blueberries
bools, marbles
bosie, bosom
brawlins, red whortleberries
breeks, breekies, little breeches
breid, bread
brichtest, brightest
broch, ancient dry-built circular
   Pictish house or castle
brod, nail
brose, oatmeal steeped in hot water
busses, bushes
but-an'-ben, two-roomed cottage
byne, tub

ca', drive, force
ca'in' (a rope), turning
cadger, hawker
caller, fresh
carl, man or lad
carlin, woman
cassies, cassie stanes, causeway stones,
   pavement
cattie, pussy cat
caun'le, candle
champers, mashed potatoes
champit, chappit, mashed
chapping, knocking
chessies (see *conkers*), chestnuts
cleek, a large hook
cleuch, cleugh, cliff
clew, ball (such as of string)
close, an outer passageway between
   shops or houses, leading to rear
   premises
clype, to tell tales
cogie, wooden vessel bound with
   iron bands
cole, haycock
conkers, chestnuts
cookies, soft buns
coorie, to snuggle
craa, crow
cracks, talks, conversations, chats
creel, fish basket
cried, called, shouted
cundies, shop gratings

curchie, kerchief
curd, the cheese part of milk (whey being the liquor)
curry t'ing, to snuggle

dae the like, do the same
dainty dame, fastidious lady
day, the, today
deen, done
diddle, to sing without words as an accompaniment to dancing
doo, dove, pigeon
dookin', doukin', ducking
dorty, finicky, petted, peevish
dub, puddle
dyke, drystone wall

e'en, eyes

fan, fand, found
farden, farthing
fause, false
fegs, exclamation meaning 'well, well', 'indeed', etc.
finn, find
fired, cooked on an open fire
fit an' a hauf, foot and a half
fite, white
flair, flairie, fleir, floor
fleggit, frightened
flegsome, fearsome
flie, fly
flittin', moving from one place to another

gab, mouth, back-chat
gar, cause, force
gear they win, money they earn, possessions earned
gif, if
gin, if, until (*gin I win*, till I get)
gird, iron hoop
girded cogie, wooden vessel bound with iron bands
girdle, griddle
girn, whine, grumble
glegness, alertness
Glesca', Glasgow

glourin', glaring, scowling
gouden, golden
gowped, gaped
grat, wept
grauppit, gripped
greetin', weeping
grice, little pig
groat, small coin, tiny shell
grossets, gooseberries
grue, fright
guddlin', fishing with the hands groping under stones or banks
guid or *gweed*, good
gundy, toffee

hap an' row, cover up warmly and wrap
harrow, agricultural rake
hauf-an-oor, half an hour
headered ba', headed ball
heckle, to comb out (of flax or hemp fibres)
hid, had
hinnae, have not
houlet, owl
howked, dug
hudderkin-dunk, see-saw
hurll, a ride in any wheeled vehicle
hyst, hoist

ilka, each
ipo, upon

jouk (or *jink*), dodge

kae, raven
keeked, peeped
keelie, street urchin
kep, kepping, to catch, catching
kimmer, young woman, neighbour
kistie, small chest, trunk
kittly, tickly
kye, cows

lane, lone (*your lane*, all alone)
larachs, ruined homesteads
lauchin', laughing
leddy, lady

leistering, spearing fish
len, a loan
lether, ladder
licht, light
littlin, little one
loon, loonie, boy, small boy
loups, lowps, leaps, jumps
lum, lummie, chimney

maiks, halfpennies
Maryhill, barracks in Glasgow
meat, old Scots word for food
mell, stone
meikle ado, much to do, fuss
midder, mother
mines, mine
minnie, mother
mootie, tiny, applied to a child as a term of affection
morn, the, tomorrow (*the morn's morn*, tomorrow morning)
muckle, large
mutch, old woman's cap

nae bother ava, no trouble at all
neeps, turnips
neist, next
nieve, fist
noo, the, now
noo an dan, now and then

'oo, wool
orra, odd, extra
o't, of it
ower, over
owre, too much

parritch, porridge
Passelet, ancient name for Paisley
pawky, slyly humorous
pease, old form of peas
peat moss, bog from which peat is cut
peeny, pinnie, pinafore
peerie, little, tiny
pickle, puckle, pucklie, small quantity
piece, slice of bread and butter, or jam; musical composition
pinkie, little finger of either hand

pinnies, pinafores
pirns, purns, reels, bobbins
played dab, kept his own counsel
pletties, outside landings in tenements, landing on outside stairs
poddlers, podlies, the young of the coalfish and other small fish
poke, pokie, bag, paper bag
pooch, pocket
pooch penny, pocket money
preen, pin
pun', pound
pyot, magpie

rade, rode
raivels, tangles
reek, smoke
reid face, red face, blush
rhype, steal
rhype my poke, pick my pocket
richt, right
roke, rock
rone, gutter pipe
rowe, roll
rummel, rumble
running messages, going on errands
rype, to steal
rype ma poke, pick my pocket

sair, sore
saut, salt
sclim, climb
sheen, shoon, shoes
shew, sew
shoogs, swings
sic, such
siccar, sure
siller, silver, money in general
sin syne, since then
skellicking, shrieking
skelpit, smacked
skirl, shriek
skroos, stooks
slaes, sloes
slaties, slates, roofing
smokies, smoked haddocks
sneck, door-latch

snoukit, sniffed
soll, sill
sook, suck
soom, swim
soree, soiree, social gathering
sourock, sorrel
soutar, shoemaker
speir, inquire
speugs, sparrows
spurtle, porridge stick
staen, stone
staff, walking-stick
steen, stolen
stooks, a shock of sheaves
stookies, statues
storry rock, a stick of rock ﹅
stour, dust
stovies, stoved potatoes
supple tam, a jointed wooden toy
   figure manipulated by string
sweir, unwilling

tasht, knocked about
tatties, potatoes
tell a lee, tell a lie

thegither, together
thole, endure, bear pain, tolerate
tief, thief
tigging, tagging, touching
til, to
tine, prong or tooth of a rake
tinny, tin or enamel mug
tint, lost
tither, the other
tod, fox
traikle, treacle
tummle, tumble
tummle the cat, somersault

wantin' nails, in need of nails
warrant, to feel certain
whippie, little whip
whit wey, why
win, get
wir, our
wisna he, was he not
wrang, wrong

yestreen, yesterday
yon (sound or sight), that